LEADING SCHOOLS IN T1

PUBLIC RELATIONS, MARKETING AND DEVELOPMENT

ESSAYS IN LEADERSHIP
FOR CHANGING TIMES

Edited by **Nigel Richardson**
with **Tory Gillingham** and **Nick Pettingale**

Published for the Association of Marketing and Development in
Independent Schools, the Institute of Development Professionals in
Education, and the Headmasters' and Headmistresses' Conference
by John Catt Educational Ltd

2010

First Published 2010

by John Catt Educational Ltd,
12 Deben Mill Business Centre, Old Maltings Approach,
Melton, Woodbridge, Suffolk IP12 1BL
Tel: 01394 389850 Fax: 01394 386893
Email: enquiries@johncatt.com
Website: www.johncatt.com

ISBN: 978 1 904 724 94 0

Set and designed by
John Catt Educational Limited

Printed and bound in Great Britain
by Charlesworth Press

CONTENTS

PART THREE

About the contributors

Elisabeth Anderson is director of the Fettes Foundation. She has worked on two continents and her experience includes sales, marketing, business consulting and fundraising. For the previous 14 years, she worked for charities in California and Maine in the United States, before joining Fettes in 2007 to set up its annual fund. She is now involved with the planning of a capital campaign there to raise £25 million for new teaching facilities, a new music school and new concert hall.

Muna Ausat became a schools' marketer after selling her successful Russian language school in 2000 and returning in 2003 as part-time receptionist to her own school, Northwood College, which is a GSA day school for 820 girls aged three to 18. Since 2006 she has been marketing and communications manager there, and she is also chairman of the Northwood College Old Girls' Association, vice-chairman of AMDIS and a governor at Rickmansworth School in Hertfordshire. She is married with three sons: two currently in state schools and one at an independent prep school. She holds the AMDIS Diploma in Schools' Marketing.

Katherine Bolton runs the marketing, design and website agency Mzuri Design, which she co-founded in 2004. She was educated at The Royal School and Guildford High School. After graduating with a degree in history from Queen Mary and Westfield College, University of London, she managed a research ethics committee at Chelsea and Westminster Hospital while completing a Diploma in Management Studies at Kingston University. She worked as a freelance marketer before forming Mzuri Design, and now enjoys working with a broad range of companies across many industry sectors, including education. www.mzuridesign.co.uk

Charlie Bostock is the registrar at Uppingham School, a post he has held since September 2009. Prior to that he was at Eastbourne College, where he was a housemaster for 12 years (in three different houses), before becoming senior master and assistant head (co-curricular) for a further four years. His teaching life began at St Richards Prep School in

Herefordshire where two separate 'gap-years' were sandwiched between his own education at Ampleforth and at St John's College, Oxford, where he took both an MA in zoology and an MSc in forestry. A third gap-year that began at Eastbourne developed into an extended habit.

Tony Bretherton has led the development function at the University of Waikato (New Zealand), the University of Limerick (Ireland) and now at Wells Cathedral School (UK). He has served on the Council for the Advancement and Support of Education (CASE) Commission on Philanthropy; chaired its Europe schools' conference and taught fundraising best practice at several international conferences. Awards include the ADAPE and FINZ awards for capital campaigns over $1million. He also has experience with fundraising in the US and Asia, where he has recently established the Wells Music Society of Hong Kong as a charity supporting Wells Cathedral School. In November 2010 Tony became director of community relations at Geelong Grammar School in Australia.

Neil Croucher is the foundation director at Marlborough College, where he has been for the past ten years. Prior to that he was development director for Bristol Cathedral, and for the redevelopment of the Harbourside in Bristol, raising £50 million from private and commercial sponsorship.

Dick Davison is a senior consultant since 2005 and now head of strategic consulting at **mtm**_consulting_, which provides most of the services described in his chapter. Before that he was at the heart of the independent sector for 16 years in various roles with ISIS, ISCis and, latterly, as director of communications for the ISC where he had responsibility not only for communications with the media but for the ISC's research activities, including the ground-breaking MORI reports on 'Why and How Parents Choose Independent Schools'. He has been advising independent schools on marketing, research and communications for more than 20 years.

Tim Edge has been development director of Worth School, St Edward's Oxford and Charterhouse. He currently works at King's College School,

Wimbledon, recently described by *The Tatler* as 'the most exciting day school in London' and winner of the prestigious *Sunday Times* International Baccalaureate School of the Year Award 2009-2010.

John Eisenhammer is chairman of Quiller Consultants, a strategic communications consultancy that specialises in helping businesses, professional bodies and institutions deal with difficult and sensitive issues. He heads Quiller's schools practice, which has advised over 50 independent schools, as well as universities and other educational bodies. He completed his DPhil at Oxford in 1983 after earlier studies at the College of Europe, Bruges, and Christ Church, Oxford. His earlier career was spent as a journalist, first at the BBC and then at *The Independent*, where he held a number of positions in the UK and abroad before co-founding Quiller in 1998.

Edward Elliott has been Head of The Perse School in Cambridge since September 2008. He graduated from St Anne's College, Oxford, and worked in industry before starting his teaching career at Whitgift School. He joined The Perse in 1997, teaching geography and politics for 12 years – a period during which he was also successively head of the sixth form, director of studies and senior deputy head.

Kevin Fear has been Head of Nottingham High School since 2007. Prior to that he was deputy head, academic and marketing, at the school and was one of the first to gain the AMDIS Diploma in Schools' Marketing. Educated at Douai School and Southampton University, the earlier part of his career was spent at the King's School, Chester, where he was head of history and also in charge of the school's marketing. His 1st XI football team there won the Independent Schools' FA Cup. He is currently on the HMC Public Affairs and Public Relations (PAPR) Committee and the ISC Marketing Advisory Committee.

Sue Freestone's path to headship was an unusual one. Having graduated with a first from the Royal Academy of Music in 1976, her first post was that of director of music at North Foreland Lodge. She ran music departments for 20 years, with a short break to have two children. Having completed an MEd in educational management at Bristol University, she became Head of Sibford School in Oxfordshire in January 1997. She was chairman of SHMIS in 2002 and moved to the headship of the King's School, Ely, in 2004.

Tory Gillingham is the general secretary of the Association for Marketing and Development in Independent Schools (AMDIS), an organisation that has been promoting best practice in the independent education sector for over 15 years through conferences and events; on and off line communications and regular networking amongst its member schools. Prior to this she had spent 11 years in independent schools' marketing; eight as marketing director at Pocklington School and then three as marketing and development director at St Peter's School, York, where she spearheaded the formation of the St Peter's School Foundation.

Henrietta Lightwood is currently director of marketing and admissions at Badminton School. She began her career working as an assistant floor manager at BBC Pebble Mill in Birmingham, following her completion of a degree in performing arts; she then worked for two years in sales and marketing and undertook both PR and marketing post-graduate diplomas before travelling for two years around the world. She spent 15 years working for PR and marketing consultancies both in Bristol and London, working on award-winning campaigns for blue chip clients such as Marks & Spencer, Somerfield, Allied Domecq and Elf Oil. She won the International Young Communicator of the Year Award, as well as awards for crisis management and industry's Business to Business Campaign Award for her work on promoting *Action 2000* Millennium Bug.

Jeanette Lloyd-Stern is director of www.mlsmedia.com. She started her career working as a placement student in the business department of the British School of Brussels. After completing her business studies degree, she worked her way up to be the marketing manager and then marketing director of several American multinationals. She founded mlsMEDIA with her husband and business partner, Michael, in 1998. mlsMEDIA were the first company to create a DVD for an independent school; the first company to put video-streaming extracts on to an independent school website – and the first to create a fully interactive digital magazine for independent schools.

Christopher Massi has over a quarter of a century of development experience, spanning schools and universities from the United States to Antwerp to London. In 2007 he launched the first development office at Merchant Taylors' School, Northwood. This has gone from having zero records to a database of 11,000, and the old boys' association is in the process of merging operations into his office. The school has launched a new glossy feature magazine, an annual fund that raises over £75,000 per year, and a £7.5 million campaign for bursaries.

Ian McLean has been in the development profession for over 20 years at leading independent schools in Australia, Scotland, England and Switzerland. Born in Adelaide, he began his career in the travel and airline industry and combined this with a prominent sporting career as a first class cricketer. In 1989 he became one of the pioneers of independent school development in Australia. Since 1999 he has successfully established and managed development programmes at three leading UK boarding schools: Uppingham, Loretto and Lancing College. Since mid-2009 he has been based at the Leysin American School in the Swiss Alps. He served on the CASE Europe board from 2001-2006; was National President of ADAPE in Australia from 1996-1998; and Chairman of the IDPE from 2008-2010.

Chris Middleton is managing director of eskimosoup, a full-service marketing team based in Hull. His qualifications include an honours degree in strategic and human resource management, and a post graduate diploma. He has always worked in a customer facing or a client care environment. His company accepts that traditional marketing and advertising still works (they use these methods frequently!), but with the internet and its new technologies, he believes that things can be done differently, with great results and with added benefits for both the consumer and brand. eskimosoup specialises in delivering integrated traditional offline campaigns with engaging online marketing campaigns.

Richard Owen was educated at Oundle School and went to university to study civil engineering. Later on he completed an MBA. After two decades working in the construction industry he decided that he needed a complete change and he returned to Oundle as the newly established development director, where he has remained for the past 13 years. He has been in charge of fundraising since the birth of the Oundle School Foundation and has established a successful ongoing operation, involving programmes for all aspects of fundraising, including legacy, major donor and annual fund campaigns. During this time he has raised over £10 million in cash and significant sums as future pledges for Oundle.

Nick Pettingale is director of development at Ellesmere College and chairman of the Institute of Development Professionals in Education. He trained as a graphic designer at Derby College of Art, before running his own company specialising in branding and point of sale material for businesses across Europe. He visited friends in Ethiopia at the time of the 1985 famine, which set him on a path of fundraising and development work. After helping to establish two charities in Ethiopia and a UK-based charity focused on disadvantaged young people in the Midlands, he renewed his business career operating at board level in three national and international companies. He pioneered the Foundation at Stamford Endowed Schools before taking up his present post.

Catherine Reeve was educated at Lancing College and read English and German at London University. She has a successful track record of business development in industry and latterly education. Having worked as a consultant for 13 years in the food and retail industry, she returned to Lancing to use her acquired business skills as development officer. She has worked for the last five years specifically on alumni relations and, in her new role as development director, she still places considerable emphasis on the importance of building and maintaining these relationships.

Dr Nigel Richardson has been co-editor of all the six books published so far in this series. He was Head of the Perse School, Cambridge, from 1994 to 2008, having previously held posts at Uppingham, the Dragon

School, Oxford, and the King's School, Macclesfield. An appraiser of Heads and teachers, a governor of several HMC schools and a Syndic of the Cambridge University Press, he was also editor of the HMC magazine *Conference & Common Room* from 1999-2002. He has written history books for children and training literature for the Industrial Society, and the educational press. He was chairman of HMC in 2007, and is working on a biography of the great Victorian headmaster, Edward Thring.

Deborah Russell moved to schools' marketing after a first career in the corporate world. She is a member of the senior management team at Duncombe School in Hertford, an independent day school for over 300 two to 11 year-olds, where she is responsible for marketing and admissions. She has served on the executive committee of AMDIS since 2006; she is an affiliate professional of the Chartered Institute of Marketing and holds the AMDIS Diploma in Schools' Marketing.

Janet Smith has been in education marketing for over 20 years, first in further education, then for Barnet LA before joining Queenswood, an independent boarding and day school for senior girls in Hertfordshire, as marketing manager in 1999. Before her career in marketing, she qualified as a teacher and taught at secondary level and in FE. She has been a member of the Chartered Institute of Marketing and a Chartered Marketer since 1992, and was awarded distinction at MSc in education management in 1997.

Erica Town is marketing, communications and admissions director for the three schools that make up St Peter's York: St Peter's, its prep school St Olave's, and Clifton Pre-preparatory School. She has been in the post for four years and her role encompasses all aspects of external affairs and the marketing mix. Prior to moving into education she worked in the food industry for Cadbury's, Young's and Nestle as a senior manager in marketing, export and human resources in a wide variety of roles, some in the UK and some specialising in pan-European change projects.

Jane Vines became development director at Downside in 2007. She has worked in independent schools for many years and, with a background in sales and marketing, was fortunate to be in at the beginning as governors and Heads started to recognise the value of income generated over and above school fees. Her present post followed assignments at Monkton Combe School and Clifton College, and five years at Kingswood School in Bath where she established the development office. She is now responsible for all aspects of development for Downside Abbey and School, reporting directly to the Abbot and his trustees.

Amanda Metcalf Wells is director of PR for Schools (www.prforschools .co.uk). She has 25 years' experience as a news reporter, spanning regional newspapers, BBC Radio and TV news reporting, and she has brought that experience to the world of independent education, acting as a PR consultant in a variety of different schools over the past decade. Her consultancy also advises on crisis management and offers media training to prepare schools for the glare of media publicity, as well as running workshops for AMDIS.

Introduction

Tory Gillingham

This is the sixth volume in the *Leading Schools* series, following on from previous titles that focused on the work of Heads; Senior Management Teams; Heads of Department; Newly Qualified Teachers and those involved in Pastoral Work. The involvement of John Catt Educational Ltd as publisher, and of the Headmasters' and Headmistresses' Conference (HMC) as co-sponsor, has been a continuing feature through the series.

This particular book is co-sponsored by two organisations, which have come into existence much more recently than HMC (1869): The Association of Marketing and Development in Independent Schools (AMDIS) and The Institute of Development Professionals in Education (IDPE). Hence I write this introduction and set the scene on behalf of AMDIS, and Nick Pettingale, chairman of IDPE, draws together many of the main themes of the various chapters in his conclusion and overview. What our respective organisations can offer to schools is described in one of the final sections of this book.

There are all sorts of reasons why a book on PR, marketing and educational development in independent education has been brought together now. There is an increasing recognition of the distinctive professional and technical expertise that the practitioners of these three skills can bring to the support of Heads and schools in their central role as educators. A few Heads are naturally skilled at all of them; a greater number acquire skills in at least one of them through experience; a proportion struggle with them and/or are under-confident about their abilities in them.

Independent schools are never far from public scrutiny – for a whole variety of reasons. Educationally, these include a deep anxiety about the state of a proportion of UK maintained sector schools, and growing controversy about entry procedures to top universities and the extent to which they favour those who are already advantaged by their education. Over recent decades, schools have been placed under a raft of legal compliance requirements by successive governments.

13

Pupils and parents as consumers (the former directly via the classroom, and the latter indirectly as fee payers) have been given increased rights to challenge the quality of the service provided – and to challenge a school that withdraws that service for disciplinary or other reasons. In media terms, our schools make good copy – positively because of their high educational achievements; negatively when pupils behave thoughtlessly or recklessly.

Reputation and its management (PR, in other words) matter even more than they did in earlier times: they underpin both our marketing and our development work. Schools must work hard to win – and to retain – friends and supporters.

In schools, most of our marketing practice is (thankfully!) a world away from the highly commercial, aggressive win-at-all-costs-and-no-holds-barred style that increasingly dominates the promotion of goods and services. In contrast, wise schools act in a more measured way, continuing to eschew the temptation to produce 'knocking copy' that does down their competitors. There is a recognition within the sector that our rivals are often also our friends, and that schools, whilst competing against each other, find that unity and some solidarity and professionalism can be a strength rather than a cop-out. However, none of this reasonableness and reticence should deflect us from the challenge of marketing our schools more efficiently, more purposefully and more sophisticatedly. There is a balance to be struck.

Many schools have adjusted very quickly to some of the opportunities discussed in this book: the new world of social networking – and with it the opportunities for so-called 'viral marketing' (encouraging one's supporters to pass on positive marketing information to their friends). Some are more alert than others to the fact that even quite young pupils increasingly drive the argument when schools are being chosen.

Others lag behind in their mastery of website provision – a theme that recurs constantly throughout the chapters that follow – and in their slow or limited recognition of the value of market research. It probably goes without saying the admissions office must be well-ordered, efficient and ready to capitalise on the results that good marketing produces.

Meanwhile, in terms of educational development, in the world of tomorrow many schools will rely increasingly on income produced other than by fees. This area has become increasingly important as well as competitive in recent years.

However, ambitious schools will yearn for continuing programmes of capital improvement as they strive to maintain their role and their reputation as world-class centres of excellence. Many will also be keen to promote an increasing number of bursaries, even if the detailed requirements of the Charity Commission drawn up during the Labour government of 1997-2010 appear to be slightly relaxed (in their interpretation, at least) in the years ahead. It is highly likely that fair-minded Heads and staff, and thinking and thoughtful parents, will continue to see the merits of making the social breadth of our schools as wide as is feasible.

If they do, they will strive to move at least a little further down the path towards the needs-blind admissions policy (*ie* making it possible for any pupil to join a school, regardless of means). If major bursaries cannot be funded through fees because current parents cannot pay more, we shall have to be more proactive in finding private individuals from other constituencies as benefactors.

AMDIS and IDPE both exist to support those working in these fields. Details about each organisation are listed on page 223.

As with previous books in this series, we have encouraged writers to centre their advice on their own experience; to write as they feel. Their work has been edited with a fairly light touch: more with house style in mind than in an attempt to eliminate all areas of overlap. More discerning readers may spot interesting differences of emphasis; some significant themes recur more than once – but this is only to be expected in three areas of work so closely interlinked and which are so multi-faceted. We hope that the chapters that follow will inform, challenge and above all make you think – and that you will enjoy them, as well as benefiting from them.

Part One

Chapter 1

Public relations: a foreword

Nigel Richardson

Remember a trio of old stories, told to you when you go someone's party. You happen to work in schools; you are staying in an area that you don't know well, and many of the other guests turn out to have once been members either of St Adrian's School or Greenbourne College. It's a distinctly hearty gathering.

Over the course of an hour or so, you hear a lot of other people's memories – and you are told three separate stories by different former pupils of St Adrian's.

> Three recent leavers from Greenbourne have responded to an advert for a package tour to New York: wonderful value at just £10, including VAT and insurance.
>
> Halfway across the Atlantic, the rowing boat isn't going too fast, but the rain hasn't started yet. "Isn't this wonderful?" says the first of them, "all this sea, fresh air and exercise – it's so much better than sitting behind a desk."
>
> Then the drizzle starts and the wind begins to get up; the second rower isn't so sure. "The weather's changing; I do hope they'll fly us home," he says. At which point the third one chips in: "They didn't last year."

The second narrator has had a few drinks, and tells his story in florid terms toned down for this publication:

> Piers is quite a talented rugby player – by Greenbourne standards, at least. He has lots of friends, but even though GCSE maths modules are imminent, he hasn't done much work.
>
> "You're not nearly ready to take maths GCSE," says the

Headmaster, "you can spend Saturday working, and no rugby match against St Adrian's for you."

This results in howls of protest from the rugby staff, and a deputation to the Head from Piers' friends. The Head offers them a compromise.

"Take him away, and make him do some work; bring him back to see me on Thursday, and we'll try him on just one maths question."

Back they come on Thursday.

The Head asks the big question: "What's 2 plus 2?"

Piers thinks, at great length. The master in charge of rugby, not wanting to lose his best player from the match, whispers the answer just loud enough for Piers to hear.

"Four!" shouts Piers, triumphantly.

"Well?" says the Head to the assembled Greenbourneians.

"Please give him another chance," they reply.

The third storyteller is even more the worse for wear: his story is loudly told, with much back-slapping:

A man wearing an Old St Adrian's tie goes into a pub and sees three large men wearing Old Greenbourneian ties.

"Shall I tell you the latest joke about Greenbourne?" he says.

"I don't think that's a good idea," says the smallest of the three, who, weighing in at 19 stone, has a collar size 23.

"Why not?" asks our St Adrian's friend.

"Well," comes the reply. "I'm a black belt at judo and I'm chief bodyguard to a Russian oligarch."

"And I'm a karate expert, and I'm six foot eight," says the second.

"I do sumo wrestling and I've been 15 rounds with the world heavyweight boxing champion," chips in the third. "Do you still want to tell the joke?"

"Perhaps I won't tell it after all," says the St Adrian's alumnus.

"Why not?" asks the first Old Greenbourneian.

"Surely it's obvious," comes the reply, "I don't want to have to explain it all three times."

What do you deduce from all this? That products of Greenbourne College tend to be over-physical and somewhat academically challenged: maybe it has a reputation for turning out what one of the various school guide publications tends to call 'genial duffers' (and some rather more menacing ones, too). It appears to have an image problem – especially as even the neutrals amongst your fellow party-goers clearly enjoy the jokes, and nobody complains that they are unfair.

You might also conclude, from the boorish delivery and obvious glee with which the stories are told to anyone who will listen, that St Adrian's is being done no favours by its distinctly arrogant former pupils. The school appears to produce pupils high in academic intelligence but with rather less in the emotional variety.

So both schools have plenty of public relations work to do, in order to correct local (and maybe wider) perceptions. What is PR? Definitions of it abound, right across the world, but one good one is 'the practice of managing communication between an organisation and its various interested constituencies'.

Independent schools, like many complex organisations, relate to a wide variety of interested individuals and groups. The more obvious ones include present parents and pupils; prospective families; governors; staff; former pupils; past parents; potential donors, great and small. A wise school pays special attention to its neighbours, especially if their homes border on to its site.

It is answerable in one way or another to a variety of organisations – including the Inspectorates, the Charity Commission, and a number of agencies enforcing branches of the law. When it wants to put up a new building, it may need to woo the planners. In a different way, it interacts with exam boards, needing to convince them in times of difficulty that it does indeed run exams efficiently, and that it doesn't make appeals against results frivolously.

It would do well to form and maintain good relationships with the local and national media, and with anyone else who influences public opinion. How independent schools are seen by the electorate is something that matters far more to us than it once did. Some would argue that, despite huge efforts by many people in recent years, the sector has been seriously wrong-footed by the creeping prevalence of words such as 'posh' and 'toff', and the way in which such images stick to us.

PR builds relationships that help to establish a lasting rapport with all these interested parties. Those who promote it must know how to convey the right messages – and the right nuances within those messages – clearly and analytically to each group of its supporters, recognising that different constituencies need slightly different approaches. In an age when the black arts of 'spin' have become widely discredited, we need to be wary not to do this to excess, but in some respects doing so – putting the essential message in the best and most positive light and in the way most relevant *to that particular group* – is plain common sense.

The Head's fundraising speech to a gathering of former 1st XV members may well differ from the one he delivers to a group of alumni who are Nobel prizewinners or Fellows of the Royal Society. When speaking to parents, s/he may emphasise that the school is seeking to control costs and fee rises, yet when talking to potential benefactors, s/he will talk about the need for more bursary funding.

When publicising the plans for the large new teaching block, the parents will want to hear about the educational opportunities it offers; the campaign board will be interested in how the development office intends to attract donors for it, and the neighbours will be far more interested in its height and appearance; they and the planning authorities will be concerned about its carbon footprint and the traffic flows it is likely to create.

In many schools (especially smaller ones) the distinction between PR and marketing can be marginal, and the techniques and tools used to deliver them both may be similar. PR brochures have plenty of stylistic and practical issues in common with prospectuses (and with fundraising literature). New media and social networking can be used to promote both of them – and to highlight development, too.

That is why the part of this book designated specifically to PR is quite brief: read on, into the later chapters that comprise part two, and you will find discussion of many of the ways in which PR and marketing can be delivered and mutually sustained – at which point your school will be ready for the educational development initiatives described in part three.

PR is essentially something that is not tangible – which is what differentiates it from both marketing and development work. Some of it can be high-profile and glamorous, but much of it is day-to-day, un-dramatic, even mundane. Wise Heads know, however, that the cumulative investment of their time spent in chatting on the touchline, and holding court during the interval of the Year 10 dramatic production, pays huge dividends in the long run; so will giving a talk to the local Rotary club or attending a parent's funeral.

People don't forget, and even appearances at sad occasions can create huge goodwill long-term. The art of the scribbled postcard for small messages of thanks, congratulation and encouragement is another weapon in our armoury: in an age of almost no handwritten letters and lots of typed, impersonal emails, the personal touch counts more and more.

All this work is critically important, because it underpins all our constituent relationships. Reputation management through skilled PR represents the 'virtuous circle' of so much of what a school does: if the feel-good factor is strong and enduring; if a school's fundamental reputation is good; if people think well of it in the good times, they will be more inclined instinctively to support it when it experiences the occasional blip or crisis. Above all, they will be more likely to make the best assumptions and to draw the best conclusions from what they hear about it, rather than the worst.

Managing expectations is important, too. Whether we like it or not, even though parents have gradually become more discerning about the very limited usefulness of league tables when judging a school, these tables continue to be comparatively high-profile, easy to grasp items of information for busy parents about its performance.

A school brutally labelled 'fourth division' by a leading newspaper may in fact be doing a superb job with the type of pupil it attracts – delivering results way beyond what they would have achieved in other, more prestigious schools. But have the counter-arguments been put *proactively*; the relative achievements explained; the other successes publicised; the ground been prepared to shape the school's image away from the crude and narrow judgement based on lists of results – not just as a one-off exercise, but repeatedly over a period of years?

The public likes *confident* messages – and so do parents.

This is why many of the messages that follow have a marketing value as well as a PR one:

- We are the professionals, in partnership with you, as parents.
- We know what we are doing; our schools have been in existence for a long time; your children are in safe hands.
- Guiding and developing young human beings is not an exact science, but the way we do it is as good as it gets.
- No, we cannot *guarantee* that your child will never be (cyber)bullied, or offered an illegal substance, or even treated inappropriately by a teacher, *ever*, and any Head who says that his or her school can, is a fool – but
- We take all complaints seriously; we don't sweep problems under the carpet and we are frank with parents when problems occur.
- We don't cull weak candidates facing pastoral difficulties in order to improve league tables: it's a policy of short-term gain, but it loses you long-term friends and reputation.
- Our staff understand the pressures on you as parents, and we seek to be reasonable, but you must be reasonable with us. We want to build a good relationship with you. Yes, I expect we sometimes seem to be an infuriating lot, but we do know a thing or two, and it takes time to build up a core of top-class staff in a good school: compared to many schools, our turnover is low, with just enough new blood each year to bring in new ideas.
- Our staff work long hours and are very dedicated. (*NB*: no direct comparisons with schools outside our sector, because such glib points-scoring is a big turn off for the thinking parent): we damn well *ought* to be superb, given our selectivity, significant fee levels and other advantages.
- We have fair admissions policies, run by people whom you can actually meet.
- A good education cannot come cheap, but we really do try to offer value for money: there are cheaper alternative schools, but in

general, you get what you pay for. We don't waste money, and we monitor spending and expenses carefully.

For more philosophical parents:

- There are intrinsic values in just having an *independent* sector in education, and there are dangers arising from monopoly provision in any walk of life, especially by government.
- The independent sector has been a pace-setter, forcing government to push up standards, and to increase spending on education: Gordon Brown made a speech when he was still Chancellor of the Exchequer (March 2006) in which he conceded this very point.
- Far from being an unnatural aberration, boarding offers huge opportunities through maximum teacher-pupil contact time.
- Above all, we are not posh – even if you keep seeing in the press that photo from the 1930s of top-hatted toffs and local oiks.

For other constituencies (always with a smile, and sometimes with part of the tongue in the cheek):

- Yes, lots of people make jokes about teachers and schools; it's inevitable – a part of life. As a profession, we probably are a bit too inclined to take ourselves over-seriously; to be too slow to see the ridiculous sides of life; to talk to adults as if they were children and, in the heat of the moment, to blame the immediate mistakes that children make on to the parent to whom we are explaining them, thus shooting not the messenger but the recipient. But the school day is a very high-pressure one, and there is no bigger responsibility – or privilege – than nurturing and developing children.
- Moreover, there's a bit more to our job than people who once went to school sometimes think: Heads don't just potter around the school all day, taking assembly and marking a few books.
- We don't make unnecessary waves or dramas out of crises.
- We really do care what people in our local community think of us: the word *partnership* is no empty slogan.

And so on. All in all, has the school gone out of its way to present itself in the best possible light to its potential supporters and allies?

One of the great potential pitfalls of the books in this series (I regularly remind myself) is to assume that we have little to learn from past generations; that styles and values can be judged across eras that are essentially different; that our predecessors made avoidable mistakes and that we know better; that they had as much freedom of manoeuvre and as many resources as we now enjoy. Even bearing in mind all those warnings, two descriptions of yesteryear, which I have carried with me through much of my career, continue to preoccupy me.

The first is Anthony Sampson's description of the public school Heads in his book *Anatomy of Britain* (1962). This was an era when running a school became exceptionally demanding, as the Swinging Sixties challenged so many hierarchies and social assumptions simultaneously:

> The isolation of the public schools is enhanced by their rulers, the headmasters. These are awesome and formidable men, whom no ex-public school boy can contemplate in tranquillity; wielding immense power, maintaining exact if sometimes irrelevant standards ... figures of massive integrity and moral uprightness ... their way of life combines monasticism with worldly ambition ... insulated against the outside world ... surrounded by inferiors, both masters and boys. Most of the major headmasters are sons of schoolmasters, clergymen or civil servants, and several are the sons or brothers of headmasters... An extraordinary number of them have won the Porson Greek Prize at Oxford, and none of the top ones are scientists...

The second is a somewhat mischievous picture of Heads and pupils, penned by the late Dr John Rae (Head Master of Westminster, 1970-86) as the loads-a-money, yuppie culture gathered momentum:

> The schools reflect the priorities of the age: every man ruthlessly for himself in the competition for good A levels, a good university, a well-paid job, and a red Porsche to roar up the school drive, scattering your former teachers like nature's rejects in the great race of life... The

26

headmasters are made uncomfortable by the thrusting financial ambition of many of their pupils, but they speak of the old boy who is earning a six-figure salary in the City in much the same tones of pride that they once used for a top scholarship at Oxford or a century for England. They would like to invite a missionary to address the sixth form, but they settle instead for a well-paid yuppie, because that way they can guarantee an audience...

You can argue, of course, that we now live in very different times; that the world has moved on; that schools are much more aware of the need to win friends and influence people; that we are more friendly towards our visitors; that things have got much better in PR terms; that the world sees us more positively.

But *are you sure*? If you aren't, there is still plenty of PR work to be done, to explain to our widest possible public all the good things about our schools. Never assume that the world knows about our successes and no longer needs to be informed or reminded about them. If *we* don't remind people about them, and explain ourselves to our friends, nobody else will.

And, as John Eisenhammer explains in the next chapter, you can never afford to be complacent...

Chapter 2

PR in a crisis

John Eisenhammer

It can take years, even decades, to build and entrench a reputation for excellence. It can take just days, sometimes even hours, for all that painstaking effort to be destroyed. This warning may be oft-stated, but it lacks nothing in relevance and urgency. A cursory look at the newspapers or the television on most days will reveal huge pressures on the reputations of companies, professional bodies and individuals in many walks of life.

For a long time schools considered themselves to be rather like island communities, somewhat removed and shielded from the rigours and intrusions of the outside world. There may be vestigial elements of this today, but overall the reality is very different. The cultural and social context in which today's Head operates has changed, resulting in very different attitudes and expectations.

Problems at schools have become newsworthy. Parental dinner party chat has lost none of its fascination with the reputations of schools allegedly 'on the up' or 'on the slide', fuelled by rising fees and a proliferation of gossipy guides to schools. All independent schools are affected by the media appetite for stories about 'toff' schools and their scrapes and peccadilloes. The immediacy of the 24-hours news cycle can give schools much less time to gather their thoughts and prepare responses.

Dealing with teaching staff is different in today's corporate culture where people 'know their rights' and where the threat of an employment tribunal hangs over every Head, however well meaning. Pupils today are also a different breed. They are more knowing and less deferential. Some are more than happy to earn extra pocket money selling stories and photographs to local and national media about goings-on inside the school.

IT departments at schools which can monitor pupil email traffic in a crisis have been shocked at the way in which national newspaper journalists, chasing a particularly sensational story, ask pupils for information or photographs with promises of substantial amounts of money. Social networking sites spread rumours and gossip, sometimes unintentionally, like wildfire.

Every Head has a story about parents from hell. Pushy parents are one thing. Litigious parents, often those with more money than sense, are a very different kettle of fish. Sadly, these are becoming more common, requiring much patience, extreme care and sound judgement while handling them (and their lawyers). Finally, there is the curse of the computer, whether in the form of pupils hacking into confidential school information or pornography suddenly appearing on a teacher's laptop.

It is a pretty safe bet that every Head will, in the next few years, face problems to do with one or all of the following:

- computer porn;
- inappropriate relationships between pupils and staff, possibly in contravention of the Sexual Offences Act 2003;
- staff litigation;
- parent litigation.

When a crisis hits, it is horrible. It invariably happens at a bad time – the call from a Sunday newspaper late on a Friday afternoon! A Head can feel very lonely very quickly. Colleagues defer rather than act decisively in support. Governors are suddenly not there, or start to meddle unhelpfully. Confusion and procrastination are too often the consequence.

How a Head grips the situation from the outset can make all the difference in preventing a drama turning into a full-blown crisis. Schools do not have the resources of big businesses, but they can, and should, take crisis management seriously. For what is at stake is nothing less than a school's greatest asset, its reputation. It is often the early decisions that prove influential in shaping the scale and eventual impact of a problem. Make the right decisions quickly and there is a good chance of containing and managing the problem.

Many Heads find it difficult to overcome their natural antipathy to engaging expert advice straight away from education lawyers and communications consultants. Some will get away with it, but many bear the scars of trying to get by on the cheap, with the wrong sort of lawyers and no communications help. It can end up costing the school a great deal more, both financially and in terms of reputation.

With this in mind, let's look at three case studies, based on situations not unlike ones that many Heads will already have experienced and that every school should be prepared for.

Case study one

It is Thursday evening, early in the summer term at St Ethelreds, a mixed boarding school for children aged 13 to 18. Supper was rather good and you are now debating whether to have a second shot of an excellent raspberry *eau-de-vie* given to you recently by a Swiss parent. The phone rings. It's Seamus, the head of IT, sounding flustered.

He has been upgrading staff laptops. In the process he has seen some emails and images, saved in the personal files of the housemaster at School House, which don't look right. These include some very familiar correspondence between the housemaster and a 17 year-old female pupil. There are also pornographic images that have been downloaded.

The head of IT says he has just found this out and has not spoken to anyone. He proposes to come over right away with the laptop. At a quick glance, the material looks serious. The images are clearly pornographic, the subjects are young and some appear to have been downloaded from a website. The email traffic is worrying, suggesting the housemaster and the pupil are, or have been, in some sort of physical relationship.

The housemaster has a long and distinguished career at the school, is respected in the common room and liked by parents and pupils. Fifty-nine years-old, he seems to be happily married, has had two children at the school, and is retiring at the end of the summer term. There has never been a hint of inappropriate behaviour.

You are distraught by what you have just seen. You like the housemaster very much, indeed he is a friend. You impress upon the IT head the importance of not saying a word to anyone, and bid him goodnight. You decide that the second raspberry *eau-de-vie* is now very much needed. So what do you do next?

There are two elements to consider here. The first is to ensure that you recognise any potential legal issues and the second is to manage your communications. At least one, possibly two, criminal offences have been committed – potential child pornography and a potential liaison with a pupil.

The first thing you must *not* do is speak to the housemaster. Your first calls that evening would be to the person in charge of child protection at school; the chair of governors; possibly the deputy head, and your lawyers.

The next morning, social services will be notified. They will almost certainly call a strategy meeting and notify the police. The police will tell you not to say anything to anyone. Events following a strategy meeting are likely to move quickly, with the housemaster suspended, his laptop confiscated, his home searched. In all probability he will be arrested. The pupil will be a witness to a criminal offence as well as the focus of your pastoral (and her parents' pastoral) concern.

The legal requirements will drive most of what you do and say. But you must decide at an early stage on a communications strategy. Staff, parents and pupils are very soon going to want to know where the housemaster is. In addition, once the police are involved, there is a chance that the matter will be leaked to the local media.

In a case involving child protection issues and potential criminal proceedings, there is not much you can say. But "no comment" is hardly ever the best response. You can be brief with the media, but you cannot give staff and parents the brush-off. You will need to say a little more. Clearly, specific circumstances will decide the precise wording, but you would probably want to confirm that X has been suspended; that matters have been referred to the relevant authorities and that it would not be proper to say any more while it is the subject of a police investigation.

It is important in any crisis to keep in mind all your audiences. What you say to one should be broadly consistent with what you say to others. Clearly, your core audiences – staff, parents – are always uppermost in your mind. Of course you will also need to be prepared to respond to media enquiries. But there may be other constituencies to consider, such as old boys and girls, donors, regulatory bodies *etc.*

You need to ask yourself which groups could be affected by hearing about the specific events at the school. It may be that it is better that they hear from you first, and in the manner in which you wish to set out the facts, rather than picking up a different version from the media or the jungle drums. You may want, therefore, to liaise closely with the police and social services about what to say, when and to whom.

Schools are small communities. Word gets around fast. Unless you are dealing in strict confidence with members of your senior management team, you should assume that whatever you write or say is a matter of public record. When you are drafting a letter to parents, think in terms of how happy you would be to see some of your words repeated back to you from the pages of a newspaper. Particularly in a situation like this one, where your lawyers will be driving much of the proceedings, you should guard against giving the lawyers too much sway over your communications with your core audiences.

While there will be limits to what you can, and cannot, say, you need to be guided by your common sense about how you talk about matters. Complex legalese can be very dehumanising. Yet the situation you are dealing with is a human drama at a number of levels. The tone and the words you use can be crucial in keeping staff onside and easing parental concerns.

With your housemaster suspended you will need to explain, within the limits of what you can say, what is going on. You will need to tell staff, and you would probably want to write to parents – perhaps not to all of them, but to those in the house and classes taught by the suspended housemaster.

As part of your early communication with parents, you may well have a sentence on the school's child protection procedures and how seriously the school takes such matters. It should be part of your prepared Question and Answer crib sheet. The school in this case study may well have had good procedures and it may simply have been very unfortunate. However, it is always prudent to take a hard look at what could be improved.

'Learning the lessons' is now a trite pledge offered by cornered politicians and beleaguered public servants on a weekly basis. But it does not alter the fact that if there are changes to be made, you need to make them, for if something similar were to re-occur without anything having been done, you would find yourself in a tricky position.

How often you write to parents, and how widely, will depend on specific circumstances. However, it is usually not a good idea to think you can get away without saying anything, hoping no-one will notice. Some elements of the events in this case study will be common knowledge. For parents of children in the house, or in classes taught by the suspended staff member, you owe it to them to say something, however brief.

In reality, few parents would go to the lengths of getting in touch to ask why they have not heard anything. But that does not imply that they do not care. Most affected parents would place a question mark over a Head who refuses to communicate with them on a matter affecting their children's education and welfare.

Check list
- Do you know who would handle such a crisis? Who would the core team be?
- Have they had relevant training, including child protection training?
- Have you got everyone's numbers to hand?
- Do you have an early warning system for possible crises?
- Have you established close links with local police, social services and any other appropriate agencies?
- Do you have the numbers of the local/national press?
- Do you have the numbers of the local child protection agencies?
- Does the HM's office know how to handle press calls?
- Is your physical site secure? Would people know how to handle the press if they turned up?
- Can you quickly change the school's website, should there be something that strikes the wrong chord in the light of events?
- Can the head of IT monitor email traffic to see if journalists are looking to pay pupils for information or photographs?
- Do you know whom to ring for help and advice?

Case study two
Master Algernon Brandcastle had to leave Cronberry abruptly in the middle of his A level year. He had a troubled disciplinary past. It then

emerged he was running a money-lending business alongside a betting ring. It appears that one junior, who was late in paying up on his losses on the 3.30 at Haydock, had been threatened.

Sir Cosmo Brandcastle QC took the news badly. An old Cronberry boy, he had put three sons through the school and expected a bit more understanding. He convinced himself the school had failed properly to follow procedures, and had acted unfairly and disproportionately regarding his son who, he believed, was a victim of a wider breakdown in pastoral care at the school. Having failed to get redress at appeal, and not got much mileage from letters to Ofsted, the Secretary of State for Education and others, Sir Cosmo decided to up the ante.

Earlier, the bursar, in a perhaps ill-judged move, had begun proceedings against Sir Cosmo for significant fees owed. Sir Cosmo issued counter proceedings for damages and took his version of events to the media. A leading national daily ran a series of lurid pieces about a school where the Head appeared to have lost control. Master Algernon, pictured looking like a saintly version of a male model, spoke of his love for the school and his grief that things had come to this.

Reporters have been spotted around the school trying to talk to pupils, and the head of IT has intercepted emails from papers offering money for stories. Parents and staff are wondering what is going on.

So what do you do?

In such a situation, legal and communications advisors need to work hand in hand. The lawyers are confident that the school correctly followed procedures. While there is usually a sensible discussion to be had about settling before getting as far as the court, in this situation the die was cast – the case is going ahead and the media are having a field day.

This is one of the toughest tests of a Head's mettle. The urge to respond; to justify; to correct grossly one-sided, sensationalist and inaccurate reporting, is huge. But this must be resisted – for now. A school, thinking about its reputation, sometimes needs to play a longer game. In dealing with pupils, it should be seen to be behaving properly, respecting confidentiality and due process, even in the face of gross provocation.

At the outset, the Head needs to have a short line to take with the media, parents and staff. While pointing out that it does not comment on disciplinary matters regarding individual pupils, the statement should give an indication of the school's thinking, making the point that even if others don't know how to behave, Cronberry does.

The reason for holding this difficult line, in this particular example, is that once court proceedings begin the rules of the game change. The school's case against the expelled boy becomes a matter of public record. This can be the moment for some aggressive management of the media. The aim is not about getting one's own back – satisfying as this may be – but about redressing the balance in the court of public opinion. While the Head retains a dignified silence, it can be useful to have someone helping the media to find, and to understand, the more interesting and colourful aspects of the proceedings.

Clearly the school should be prepared for all eventualities, but in a case like this, if the lawyers have done their homework, the court should find against a parent who has more money than sense. The school needs to be ready with its communications – briefing staff, writing to parents and issuing a press statement, so that everyone understands not just what has happened but also receives some key messages about the school, its values, what it expects from its pupils and how it looks after their best interests in the widest sense.

The school should appeal to the instincts of parents, and newspaper readers, most of whom probably do not approve of the behaviour of Sir Cosmo and who understand the importance of respect for authority and the need to behave in an acceptable manner in a special community like a boarding school. The tone needs to be one of more in sorrow than in anger, and the content clear in its understanding of what is right and what is wrong.

Particularly when dealing with one 'mad' parent, Heads must not lose their faith in parents as a whole. All our experience tells us that most parents are sensible people. They know that things go wrong in the real world; that things are sometimes messy. It is how you deal with the mess that will define perceptions of you as a Head. A well-handled crisis, preventing it from turning into a disaster, can win plaudits and respect. It can be the making of a Head.

Case study three

Bertha Sanchez is a part-time, peripatetic yoga teacher at St Guinevere's High School for Girls. She has held a couple of classes a week for a number of years, and is well known and popular amongst parents. She is not employed by the school. She has been CRB checked, although no-one can quite remember when.

With hindsight there were a few things that should have been warning signs. A 15 year-old pupil had gone to warn her housemistress over concerns about the friendship between a friend of hers and Ms Sanchez. But the girl clammed up, refusing to name names and gave nothing for the housemistress to go on. She did mention it to the Head. The Head used the occasion to remind, in a general way, Ms Sanchez of her duty of care.

Several years later the Head had to stop a yoga away-weekend that Ms Sanchez was organising that lacked adequate supervision. Then, in the intervening period, the Head retired and a new broom took over.

In the middle of one summer term, a few more years on, Ms Sanchez disappeared. The next thing the school heard was that she had been arrested, and charged with sexual relationships with young people in her care.

The police had been tipped off by a jealous former lover who had found letters. They indicated that Ms Sanchez had had a sexual relationship with the young pupil who, all those years ago, had gone to her housemistress about her concerns for a 'friend'. She had been trying to talk about herself.

By now she was at university, but had agreed to appear as a witness in the trial at Ashford county court in two months. The school has co-operated fully with the police who have plenty to go on and are not that interested in involving the school in any direct way.

So what do you do?

At first sight, this may seem similar to the first study, but there is an important difference: the effect of the passage of time, which means that this case involves an adult former pupil, rather than a current one.

In co-operating with the police you will have got legal advice and you will have gone thoroughly over the history of how the school dealt with those earlier warning signs.

It is fortunate that the police do not appear to be that interested in the school. You have met the former pupil who will be a witness at the trial. She appears to be very sensible, wants to keep her involvement to a minimum and bears no grudge against the school.

Against this background, your communications handling comes down mainly to a choice. Do you swear your senior management team to secrecy and hope the trial goes off without anyone noticing? Or do you decide that the chances are so great of something coming out that it is better to tell parents and staff in your own words?

Each case must be decided on its own merits. But experience suggests that in a situation like this it is better to opt for the latter course. These sorts of cases have many of the ingredients that the media love. The chances are that even before it comes to court a journalist will have been tipped off by the police. When the call comes and the story emerges, you are left scrambling to deal with 'facts' out of your control.

It usually makes sense to get on the front foot, preparing your plan of action so that, as soon as you know the trial is going ahead, you brief staff and write to parents with a concise letter that informs, reassures and heads off further questioning by saying that the legal case restricts what you can say.

Once a verdict has been handed down, you should again, for the sake of completeness, let parents and staff know the outcome; that this has been a distressing time for the young woman and that everyone is now looking forward to moving on.

Top tips

- Get legal and communications advice working hand-in-hand and take advice early.
- Show leadership and act fast – time is not on your side: media deadlines will not wait for leisurely decision-taking and debate.
- Establish the facts – all of them: ask all the awkward questions and keep pressing.
- A cover-up is worse than the original offence.
- Don't fudge. Err on the side of clarity of message.

- Always tell the truth – but not necessarily the whole truth.
- Aim to get it over with – one media hit is better than days of painful coverage.
- Remember all your audiences.
- Know your legal options – but do not be hidebound by the law: use common sense.
- Have your systems in place – numbers, advisers, *etc*. Know who your core crisis management team would be.
- Prepare for the worst, and rehearse.

I could, of course, have cited many more case studies – for example, those involving the selling and acquisition of drugs; or behaviour by pupils deep into the summer holidays that is likely to bring the school into disrepute. There can be no hard and fast rules about whether or not a school under pressure should seek professional PR help with its crisis management.

In the scale of many items in a school's budget, such assistance does not come cheap and, as with most professional advice, you tend to get what you pay for in terms of quality. If you do decide to go down this route, however, you should be supplied not only with expert technical help and experience about how the media works, but you should gain the support of a listening, dispassionate but concerned ally, of a type whom Heads so often lack at lonely times of crisis.

Finally, to return to two points already made:

- It can take years, even decades, to build and entrench a reputation for excellence. It can take just days, sometimes even hours, for all that painstaking effort to be destroyed.
- Many Heads find it difficult to overcome their natural antipathy to engaging expert advice straight away from education lawyers and communications consultants. Some will get away with it, but many bear the scars of trying to get by on the cheap, with the wrong sort of lawyers and no communications help. It can end up costing the school a great deal more, both financially and in terms of its reputation.

Can you afford such advice? Can you afford *not* to have it?

Part Two

Chapter 3

Marketing and admissions: a foreword

Nigel Richardson

Remember another old story. The chairman of the governors has commandeered the marketing director and the recently-arrived young Head for a walk around the school grounds in the half-hour or so before the Head's first prize-giving.

The chairman is an old hand at prize-givings, so he has decided to spend this short expedition outlining to the other two his vision for the school for the next ten years. The marketing director is happy to go along with his idea, but the Head seems understandably reluctant and pre-occupied: he has been in post only for a few weeks, and he would much rather be reading over the speech he is about to give than going on this impromptu walking-lecture-tour.

Suddenly they realise that they haven't given themselves enough time to get round the lake and back to the Great Hall. The chairman, ever a man of action, doesn't hesitate. He strides straight off across the water, and arrives on the other side, completely dry. The marketing director breaks off from talking to the Head and follows the chairman to the other side. Again, not a drop of water – even on the sides of her shoes.

From the opposite bank they both watch as the Head takes a very tentative step into the water and disappears beneath the surface. The bubbles stop. Silence.

"I thought you were telling him about the stepping stones," says the chairman.

"What stepping stones?" replies the marketing director.

I've heard many versions of this anecdote – not only with people of different gender allocated each part in the cast, but also with the walk-on-water role allocated variously to Heads, deputies, bursars, development directors or whoever suits the moment. For the purposes of this chapter, however, it's the marketing director who gets to be the star.

Why? Because the ability to work miracles; to achieve the impossible; to do so whilst keeping a calm exterior and sense of humour are especially important at a time when many schools face increasing competition from rivals in both sectors; when rising costs and rising fees are an ever-present concern; when economic downturn can threaten staff jobs and ultimately (if a school faces closure) cause huge disruption to pupils' careers.

Even for successful and thriving schools, market research, a long-term marketing strategy and the day-to-day act of good marketing itself have become requirements that few schools can ignore. As they say in many businesses: to stay still is to go backwards.

The stakes are high. Just as it is true that elections in the UK are mostly decided by the actions of a fairly small percentage of floating voters, so it is true within our schools. Deficit or surplus, health or extinction, is often determined by the floating or first-time buyers: those with no obvious emotional or other reason to join our particular school. These are the people whom we have to impress. We have to know who they are; how to reach them and what messages to dangle in front of them.

The pressure was not always like this. Go back through the archives of many schools and you will find brief, black and white prospectuses, with never a DVD nor a web-link in sight. Marketing was one of many jobs that the Head managed to squeeze in between teaching and cricket-watching. For many, *marketing* was a concept which did not exist as such – and there was certainly no marketing 'department'.

In 1853, the great Victorian Headmaster, Edward Thring, found himself in charge of a school with the potential to benefit from the railway age, but one whose nearest station was three miles away. Time and again in the years that followed, he made the walk from station to school and back again with prospective parents, working off his own nervous energy in the process.

As one contemporary put it: 'Having had their valises loaded on to a trap, he would trudge back with them to Uppingham, his sheep-dog at his side, no doubt expounding to them with infectious enthusiasm his principles of education.' In building up a tiny local grammar school into a nationally-known boarding school of 300+ pupils, although he proved that he was no mean marketeer, meeting people in such circumstances was, for him, not a science: it was simply a part of daily life.

Remarkably to us, in Thring's day many parents who heard of a Head who inspired them were prepared to send their sons (and less often, their daughters) to schools far from the family home, visiting them only rarely. Even more then than now, marketing was done by word of mouth: Thring built up a huge network of Uppingham families around Liverpool and Manchester, many miles away from his school in the East Midlands.

Generation after generation of the same families supported many such schools, as sons followed fathers (and again to a lesser extent, daughters followed mothers). Even during the dark days of the 1930s Depression, when some schools down-sized and others closed, the archives suggest that many schools had little real preoccupation with marketing as such.

Thring and the successive generations of Heads worked in an era when 'tribal' loyalties were often very strong. How different it all is for many of us nowadays! Very few schools have anything resembling a national catchment. Parents (laudably and understandably) set a high store by being able to support their children in matches, plays and concerts – and time pressures on adults mean that whole days spent travelling to do this are an impossibility. At the same time, increasing numbers of parents scrutinise exam results and – however much they may deny it and others regret it – league tables too. They compare fee levels; they demand value for money, and they choose schools accordingly.

All these things present new challenges to schools: how to be distinctive despite the ever-increasing demands of national exams and the pressures to gain a 'good' university place. In facing them, schools are increasingly striving to do four things.

First, they compete ever-more strongly with each other within their traditional or existing markets, for pupils whose parents have become much more searching and sophisticated in their assessment of the choices on offer. While prep school Heads play a big part in influencing school choice at the age of 13, they do not ultimately determine it: parents do. That said, at earlier age-groups – for example, three-plus and four-plus – the market is essentially parent-led, although after half a century in which child-centred education has been the prevailing fashion (for good or ill), thereafter it is pupils themselves who play an increasing part in the decision.

When I became a secondary school Head in 1994, school choice seemed to be pupil-led only at 16+: by the turn of the millennium it had become more and more so at 13-plus and 11-plus; by the time I left the school in 2008, I felt it was a growing trend at nine-plus and seven-plus. You may remember the response of the parent asked by a boarding school Head if his child wanted to come to the school: "Headmaster, when I want to put my dog into kennels, I don't ask it which kennels it wants." There aren't many of that type (or should it be 'breed'?) of parent around these days.

Secondly, schools seek to broaden and expand the market in new directions. Times may not be easy, but many people still aspire to join independent schools. Some parents are new to the sector; others want to recreate the schools they themselves remember – including those whose schools had what many call a 'grammar school ethos', especially if they grew up in Northern Ireland. According to figures from the Independent Schools' Council (ISC), 50% of UK parents would like to be able to afford places in our schools; 25% of maintained sector teachers would like to send their children to them and 40% of our parents are first time buyers. How do we reach *them*?

Thirdly, schools wrestle with methods of marketing and communication unknown to earlier generations. They have to ensure that their marketing messages are the ones that survive the regular household cull of mailshots, prospectuses and DVDs; that their names are the ones that appear at the top of the Google list; that their websites are eye-catching and regularly updated and redesigned, telling people things they want to know about.

Finally, schools face increasing challenges to retain, as well as to recruit. It is highly significant that although the independent sector educates only about 7% of the nation's children at any one time, 14% of pupils have been in independent education at some time in their lives. Parents are much more prepared to mix and match between sectors (for example, moving their children into sixth form colleges – see chapter 9), especially if they have more than one child's fees to pay. They also face a combination of rising taxation, pension and healthcare pressures and the prospect of sharply-rising university fees.

Parents are also increasingly prepared to consider different schools for different children – and whereas it was once fathers who tended to make choices about schools, mothers (highly educated themselves, and many of them now earning as much, if not more, than fathers) are also completely involved in the decision-making. Ignore social networking websites such as mumsnet at your peril...

So we can't take anything – or anyone – for granted. Schools have to promote themselves far more assertively, taking traditional constituencies much less for granted. What does this mean in practice? Key messages have to be identified and promoted. Some of these will be well-tried and successful; when those of my generation, whose children have passed through education and are now in the 20s or 30s, are tempted to think that these messages sound tired or predictable, we should remind ourselves that for *every* generation of new parents, some things are crucially important, just as they once were for us. These important things include academic challenge and good pastoral care.

However, one of the biggest technical challenges for schools involves finding fresh new ways to express old ideas. How do you make traditional values remain eye-catching 'big ideas', rather than clichés, or things that every parent assumes we provide anyway? The poet W B Yeats believed that 'Education is not about filling buckets: it's about lighting fires'. G K Chesterton defined it as 'Simply the soul of society as it passes from one generation to another'. In our own time, Chief Rabbi Sir Jonathan Sacks has written that: 'There are two different battles for freedom. One is fought by soldiers, the other by teachers, and it is the second that eventually determines the course of history. The world we build tomorrow is born in the lessons we teach today.' I've always felt that there was wisdom and attraction in the idea (variously attributed) that: 'The purpose of a liberal education is to make one's mind a pleasant place in which to spend one's time.'

You will be able to think of similar memorable phrases, strap-lines and slogans for yourself. But while you try to do so, will you also remember the famous *Mastermind* spoof by the Two Ronnies in which Corbett's answers were always one behind Barker's questions? Too often our marketing is like that: stories change fast, making today's newspapers into tomorrow's fish and chip wrapper. In a similar way, this September term's detailed parent-preoccupations may be quite different from those that were prevalent in the last days of June.

Meanwhile, how does one know what is going on parents' minds at any given time? Too few governing bodies hold parents' forums to explain their aims and decisions, and to listen to what parents want to tell them. Talk to your Parents' Association committee about the concerns and ambitions of their fellow-parents. Study the superb ISC daily bulletin service to the full. As a Head I read it every day (and I still do); I made sure that it was passed on via our intranet to the whole of my senior management team – but looking back, we never really discussed or analysed it as a guide to our marketing. I think we missed a trick: parents read a newspaper or two *every day*: they are bombarded with messages – often gloomy – about the state of education, and their brains engage on these messages when they visit prospective schools.

If your marketing succeeds in getting people to contact you, a different set of challenges then arises. Are your staff in reception sufficiently customer-friendly? Whenever I go to a school to appraise a Head, I try to find an excuse to sit for a while within earshot of reception: it can be very revealing.

Is there a clear map of the school on the website? Are there prominent display signs at the gate? Society has become far less top-down in recent years: does our site signage reflect this informality? Is it part of the brand identity? Or is the visitor greeted by an overkill of health and safety warnings, and a lot of bossy rules? 'No entry: no parking on the drive: no speeding, no smoking (no breathing?).' And where is the word '*please*'? After all, we expect our pupils to use it.

Who does the parent tours in your school? Does the Head have delusions of indispensability in this respect? Prospective parents like to meet *pupils*, or at least someone who is not over-schooled in marketing techniques. An increasing number of them (at least, at secondary level) wonder if a Head doing tours him/herself betrays a misplaced sense of time-priorities.

Tour guides need to know where to take visitors, but their answers to questions mustn't be too rehearsed and un-spontaneous. The mechanisms for making sure that tour guides turn up must be fail-safe: hiatus and confusion are not a good situation in which to create friendly introductions and good first impressions.

Then, after the tour, what messages do visitors receive as they cross the threshold into the Head's study? Remember that earlier quote from Anthony Sampson (chapter 1). Are we *sure* that we've done all that can be done to shed that fusty and forbidding old image? A depressing number of parents have bought the media line that all independent schools are posh – and another group has stomachs that seem to tighten up as we greet them – perhaps suddenly recalling some perceived injustice from their own schooldays, or maybe some guilty secret that their school never found out about.

We need to put them at their ease. The black gown on the back of the door is just as likely these days to be seen as intimidating one-upmanship than as a sign of academic pedigree. Are there comics or books for younger siblings to read (and bring into the study with them)? We need to make them welcome too – unlike the receptionist at a hotel in South Africa who, when asked the question: "Do you take children?" replied without obvious irony: "No sir, only cash or credit cards."

How much do Heads talk to prospective *children*? When I was a prospective parent myself, I was amazed at the Heads who completely ignored my children. So, once I became a Head, I learned to tell my own adult visitors that I would more or less ignore them, while I asked their 11 year-old about his maths, or the science experiment he'd just done. Most parents listened in; some claimed to have learned things they'd never been told before; I like to think that nearly all of them saw my approach in a distinctly positive light.

Be warned, however, that while you are talking to their child, the parents' eyes and attention may wander, so that they notice things in your study that you have long stopped noticing. After a successful inspection, we gave every employee a small thank-you, in the shape of a particular brand of gold labelled champagne. I kept the gold boxes, which were very useful for storing this and that, and they all got parked in a row along a bookshelf above the door into my PA's office. I stopped noticing them until one parent asked how they came to be there and, shortly afterwards, a visiting journalist from *The Independent* wrote in her article that we were a 'champagne school'.

Where retention is concerned, do schools treat *existing* parents – and, indeed, pupils – with sufficient courtesy and consideration? Are there useful lessons to be learned from how other organisations manage their clients and create 'brand loyalty' – for example, the hotel industry? Do we use parents' evenings to maximum effect, training new young staff in how to deal with those who are confused about the more eccentric aspects such as the language of independent schools? Do we teach staff how to respond to over-the-top, stressed emails? Do we ensure that reports are honest but also diplomatic, positive and friendly, with constructive ideas for the future rather than clever one-liner put-downs about the past?

We are remembered by departing pupils for the reports we write, and whilst we shouldn't evade harsh truths, some reports re-read many years later can seem unnecessarily negative or small-minded. Are we sure that newsletters, paper or electronic, give parents enough information (for example about match times and venues), but not so much that their busy lives and kitchen notice boards become overwhelmed with information?

Recent decades have brought a huge growth in the study of the process whereby consumers make choices and decisions. Opinion pollsters were unknown a century ago, and nearly six decades of commercial television have spawned a huge industry in market research and strategic planning. Can we more accurately predict future patterns of demand? What features should we advertise? Can schools do more to discover why some parents visit a school but then *don't* sign up to it, rather than merely conducting satisfaction surveys amongst those who do? What advertising is effective and what isn't?

Where should we advertise – especially if we want to attract pupils on bursaries from areas that have traditionally sent nobody to an independent school? If you use the local press, try to join with other schools to save time and money by a joint publicity campaign: estate agents hunt in packs, where advertising is concerned; for maximum impact and maximum bargaining clout over costs, we should do so, too. Concerted action by a group of schools may also enable us to ensure that school supplements in the local press appear at times of year that suit us. Supplements in mid-August may suit newspapers, but they are a poor time for schools, with so many prospective parents away on holiday. And *how* do you advertise? Too many of our box adverts are too cluttered, or too filled with independent school acronyms (IAPS, HMC, ISBA, AGBIS), which are incomprehensible to the average reader.

As a sector, have we been too wary of admitting our need for specialist support in market research? Does anyone in your school consciously spend time analysing your market: asking whether it is changing, and checking out that the assumptions of the most experienced Head are, in fact, still correct?

I confess I was sceptical about large-scale market research until my school embarked on a major expansion, whereupon the banks expected it as part of their due diligence process. I considered that I knew my market inside out. I was wrong: I learned a great deal from the skilful and sensitive questioning of parents by so-called 'mystery shoppers' not directly connected with the school (who did manage to get responses from some parents who had visited but then not chosen us); from an analysis of the local competition seen through fresh and detached eyes; from the way that experts analysed the local community and its future population patterns, broken down by postcode, year-group, types of household, income and spending habits, commuter travel patterns; public transport provision, and so on. After all, it's no use doing large-scale letterbox drops in areas where there are few children, or advertising bursaries in areas where every parent is too affluent to meet the maximum income criteria.

Good market researchers should also be able to tell you about changing patterns of local media: for example, the decline of a once-dominant local paper and the rise of free publications. They should be able to help you tailor your promotional literature so that you can do some of your own research in stage two: for example, on how people first heard about the school.

It is increasingly specialist work, with tailor-made IT packages to support it. If you can't afford it on your own, find a school within a reasonable distance with which you are not in direct competition, with which you might be able to share the cost. Maybe we are sometime too obsessed with our local rivalries to see the bigger picture. (See chapter 6.)

Many schools do prospectuses well – but there is a difference in time and cost between a revision and a complete rewrite. So it's a good idea to have a main document that has a print run of several years, supplemented by a more home-produced supplement that is updated annually. Get yourself some eye-catching flyers for doctors and dentists' waiting rooms and libraries. Consider adverts on bus shelters on key commuter routes.

Make sure that both prospectuses and flyers refer people to your website. But then the site itself must be fit for purpose, and with at least some of its material written for children rather than adults. It needs less of the bland marketing language that you can read about *any* school, and better access to detailed material that gives prospective parents a feeling that they are on the inside track of what it's like to be *actual* parents: more information that is accessible to everyone, and less of it hidden away in a secure area of the site. Most of all, there should be no references on the site in May to the 'forthcoming' carol service, which in fact took place last December.

How many sites give comprehensive information about the soon-to-arrive new Head (including a good photo)? Not nearly enough, despite the fact that the journalists often tell parents that a good Head is crucial to a good school: it was my successor's face, not mine, which was dominant on my school's website during my final few months in post. We also need sites that link up in brand identity terms with the prospectus, newsletters, *etc*; more regular revamping and restyling. More schools need to train staff in website maintenance and updating, and then to give them time to do it. It is not difficult and not excessively expensive, and it will pay dividends.

Many of these themes will be developed by our writers in the second part of this book. Above all, remember one crucial thing. There are few parents, if any, whose main priority when choosing a school is anything other than that their children should be successful, happy and fulfilled. For many years, I had posted outside my study the words of a child, which I came across in 2003 on the notice board of a special needs school in Ohio:

See what I found.
Some new corners of myself
Hiding away, tucked out of sight,
Untapped, untried, I found them
Whilst reaching out to others.
I wonder how much more of me
There is to discover.

Many, if not most, schools aim to deliver such discoveries. The challenge is: how do we convince people that we are successful in doing so – and more likely to deliver them than the rival day school down the road or the boarding school in the next county? Read on, in the hope of finding out.

Chapter 4

The media at our disposal

The prospectus, DVD and website

Jeanette Lloyd-Stern

The prospectus

The trend for today's prospectuses is to incorporate bigger and better photos and fewer words. Everyone agrees that photographs can say so much more and, as a result, in essence the printed school prospectus has become more like a photograph album.

Of course every school has pupils and every school has classrooms, so the trick is to capture the essence of the school via warm, 'up close and personal' photographs of the real characters at the school. But, as some schools spend more than £20,000 on a glossy prospectus that ultimately most families add to their pile of *me too* prospectuses and eventually throw away, one wonders whether the investment is actually worth it.

Interestingly, if you take a handful of independent school websites you will see that more than half of them now offer the prospectus as a PDF or static page turning magazine. This feeds the need for parents to have information immediately, and at the same time it saves on the exorbitant cost of printing and postage, as well as giving a very positive environmental message about the school.

A few schools have already stopped using a printed prospectus altogether, in favour of a fully-digital online interactive production. One school in this category takes readers through the school's story in the reassuring format of a magazine, but also allows prospective parents and pupils actually to experience the school through compelling and interactive animation and video testimonials from the pupils themselves.

One of the complaints about any printed prospectus has been that the moment it is printed, it is out of date. A digital format enables a school to keep its prospectus fresh by changing the content in it as often as it wishes without the heavy creative, printing and postage costs. This same method can be used for the annual (or termly) school magazines, making the content more exciting with words, photographs and video extracts from the school year. The format can then be updated every year. There is a further advantage for schools, too: unlike with printed magazines, you can actually view the readership statistics for every page, to know what content really captures your readers' interest.

Peter Anwyl, President of AMDIS, which represents more than 400 independent schools in the UK, said in January 2010 that once he had seen an interactive digital prospectus at work: "I needed no convincing that this was the way forward for those schools who wanted to communicate with their parents and alumni/ae in a modern and immediate way. It should be high on the 'to do' list of any school, as it is undoubtedly the way forward."

The DVD

There is no doubt that a good video about your school adds depth, builds familiarity and trust – and it beats photographs as a persuasive communication tool. While parents may be sceptical about the traditional prospectus-speak, video testimonials from former or existing pupils are one of the most successful marketing tools you can employ.

Good video content is therefore very successful, and now with the huge uptake of fast internet access, you can negate the need to create massive copies of DVDs – instead pushing the video content out on to your website and your blog. The great thing about video content is the wide variety of ways in which it can be used and re-edited to increase pupil registrations, raise the school's profile and raise monies for the school.

The website

The website has become the most important communication tool for any school. Designed correctly, it should both increase pupil registrations and decrease the cost of communicating with parents.

Where recruitment is concerned, buying an independent education is an expensive decision. The school website therefore needs to entice prospective viewers, either to call the school or at least to leave their email details, so that you can start an ongoing dialogue with them, to build their trust and interest.

Using the website to communicate with current parents offers you a cost-effective, dynamic tool. It is interesting to note that few schools have been brave enough to let go of the paper newsletter altogether, but some have done so with remarkable success. One, which decided over two years ago to stop printing its weekly newsletter altogether and to put the news on to its website, found that while initially there was some reticence from a very small minority of parents, it soon had 100% buy-in from parents. Its statistics show a big surge of web traffic to the school site on a Friday afternoon when the news goes up.

Your website is never ever finished and creating a new school website is only half the story. The other half is keeping it fresh with new and interesting stories. Don't be fooled into thinking that the success of your website is all down to the design, because the real success is down to your content. The uptake of Twitter and Facebook is all about user-generated content. People want to interact with your website and see information presented in a variety of ways, whether it is written material or in an audio or video format.

Most of all they want real content: not the same glossy text that you used in your prospectus, but the real life school action stories. That means that you must have an easy-to-use content management system (CMS), so that anyone who can type can also update the site and upload videos. So you must devise a system for getting people to contribute to the site internally – but one which also enables you to prevent unsuitable or unauthorised material being posted.

Your web copy needs also to be a personal communication to the individual reading it. Therefore rather than thinking that content is about the school *per se*, think of it in terms of being about the needs, desires and fears of your audience, whether they are your prospective, current, or former pupils or parents.

Your audience will not remain long on a website that is not directly focused on them. For example, most independent schools (especially at the senior age group) completely miss the opportunity to market to prospective pupils who, whilst not the purse holder, are very often the decision-makers. And not surprisingly, prospective pupils are interested in different things from those that preoccupy mum and dad...

If you have someone with a flair for writing, consider adding a blog to your website and encourage people's comments in response to it. Analyse your web traffic statistics and see what content gets the most clicks. Then you will have a blueprint for redesigning your website navigation around the interests of your audience.

For example, photo galleries are really popular on school websites. Commit to making sure your website is constantly fresh, even if you can only update one photograph every week. And of course if you say you are going to put match results up on Monday, be sure you do it – or you can be sure that you will have parents calling you!

Private areas on websites are very effective ways to get your information across about that rapidly-spreading bout of head lice. More seriously, you can really use these private areas to display every piece of information that a parent is ever going to want or ask for, rather than have them bombarding the school office staff with telephone enquiries.

You can also set up these private areas for teachers to post the homework or form news – but beware of doing this if you do not have the commitment from the teachers to update it in a timely manner. Nothing looks worse than a school site where, for example, the head of geography loves writing and updating the departmental area on the site, while the head of maths does not have the time or inclination to do it – and thus conveys the lacklustre impression that maths is a weak subject area at the school.

There is, of course, no point in having a fabulously-designed website if no one is visiting it. To drive current parents and alumni to your website on a regular basis to view your fresh content, you can use RSS feeds, e-newsletters and links from other sites such as Facebook and Twitter. For recruitment purposes, prospective families will be going to search engines such as Google to do their research on different schools.

There is a paramount need to make sure your website gets on the top page of Google and other search engines for search terms related to your school, or potential customers will not realise you exist. In today's world, you will get more return on investment from a thorough online marketing strategy to drive potential families to your website than you will from an expensive advertisement in a local magazine. And the beauty of an online marketing campaign is that it offers complete measurability.

Lastly, don't forget you must have your terms and conditions policy document governing the use of the website somewhere on that site. At a minimum, the terms of use should deal with basic disclosure obligations, include a disclaimer of liability, and provide for the licensing of the website content to users.

Working with the local media

Amanda Metcalf Wells

Why are local media important?
The local media can play a key part in spreading positive news about your school. Local newspapers are always looking for news stories within their local communities and, by establishing good working relationships with key journalists, schools can win themselves plenty of positive, free publicity.

Developing trust and building a relationship are the key requirements. One designated person within a school – usually the person responsible for marketing – needs to make contact with the local newspaper. By talking to a named journalist, a relationship can be built that is mutually beneficial.

Too often independent schools complain of bias against them or a lack of interest on the part of their local newspaper. The truth is that the vast majority of – if not all – local newspapers *are* interested. The misunderstanding comes about because all too often schools fail to understand what it is the journalist wants.

What makes news

Consider for a moment what might make news in your school. Is it the story about your choir reaching the final of a choral competition, or is it the tale about the school cook who, having battled to lose weight, runs her first marathon cheered on by pupils?

It might surprise some people to know it's much more likely to be the second story that captures the newspaper reporter's imagination. Human interest stories are always going to make good news. Think for a moment of the many human interest stories to be found in *any* school: stories about individual success for a pupil; maybe a tale about a teacher going the extra mile to bring a subject to life for his or her class; or a story about a groundsman growing vegetables, helped by young pupils learning about healthy eating.

One school or another always reaches the final of that choral competition – and there is no shortage of such events, either. It may well represent news for your internal school audience – but, alas, it is not going to whet the journalist's appetite.

How journalists work

Identifying what might make news marks the beginning phase, but to succeed in getting regular, positive coverage in the local press, schools need to develop an understanding of how newsrooms operate. Do you know when the local paper's deadlines are? Do you aim to ring the journalist whom you have got to know on deadline day, or do you wait until the following day?

If you want the best chance of getting your story noticed, make that phone call on the day that the newspaper appears on the streets. That is when the reporter and news editor begin the thankless task of planning the following week's coverage. Get your story noticed, by taking the time to make that phone call.

If you rely simply on email, your press release will have to take pot luck alongside the hundreds of releases that find their way into the news editor's inbox each and every day. Too often your work will be wasted because it has gone unseen into the delete bin.

Getting the press release right

The essence of the school's story needs to be captured in the opening paragraph of a press release. It is a bit like drawing up an advertising slogan; you want to capture your audience and make them want to read on. This is not about essay writing. Good press releases are short and snappy. There are two simple rules:

- Make sure you answer these questions: Who; what; where; why; when and how?
- Try to keep your release to just one page in length and use the opening paragraph – the 'intro' – to entice the cynical journalist.

It is a sales technique that works. If you let the release ramble, and if you use too many long phrases, you will quickly find it is deleted: consigned to the virtual waste paper bin.

The power of the photo

Every newspaper needs inspiring images. All too often stories are used principally because of the photo opportunities they present. Good press photographers can transform the dull and predictable shot of a group of pupils into an inspired and imaginative photo, taken from a different angle, maybe featuring just one pupil plucked from the group.

Schools can learn a lot from watching how the best press photos are constructed. Some media organisations will ask you to supply a photo, but many local papers prefer to send their own photographers into schools to take images, Again, it is important to have spoken to a reporter or picture editor to find out how s/he works.

Using broadcast media

Local radio is often overlooked by schools, but busy radio newsrooms will be interested in many of the press releases that make news for the local paper. BBC local radio tends to cover more news than its commercial equivalent, but both are worth talking to, in order to find out what might interest them. A press release alone will not be enough for the radio reporter. S/he will want to record a short interview with the Head, or with a pupil at the centre of the story.

Not just radio: what about regional television too? The BBC's early evening regional programme, which goes on air at 6.30pm each weekday, will often cover school stories. The ITV equivalent, which is on air from 6pm, will also feature newsworthy stories about education from a regional perspective. Maybe your Head would be prepared to speak on a national issue? Regional TV newsrooms are always on the lookout for spokesmen and women who will comment on matters that are making national news.

The best way to get either radio or TV coverage for your school is to watch the regional news programmes to gain an insight into the sort of stories they cover. Ring the newsroom when you have a story that you think may interest them. The TV reporter will want to record interviews in much the same way the radio reporter does, but for TV the story also needs moving images.

Updating the school website

Do not forget about the school's own website when you are spending time considering what might interest the local media. The stories that feature in your press releases should also be displayed prominently in the Latest News section of the school's website.

This sounds obvious, but for too many schools Latest News might just as well read News Which Is Way Out-of-date. Parents and prospective families do not want to see the website's home page featuring a Christmas Nativity story in June.

You should aim to update these Latest News entries weekly. If that sounds onerous, encourage heads of department, or responsible pupils, to create their own entries – although someone should act as the school's official gatekeeper to the site, in order to avoid unauthorised and mischievous additions and amendments.

Remember, the website is a shop window that should reflect *everything* that goes on in school. It is a potent way of allowing the outside world to take a glimpse into the heart of a school. One of the easiest ways to capture the breadth and range of what goes on is to make sure that the news areas are regularly updated.

* * * *

Social media and social networking

Chris Middleton

Online social networking is not going away!
No other generation has lived and documented life as much as this one, from sharing party snaps to rating the status of your individual actions and even communicating the most private of thoughts. Most of life's dramas are, it seems, being documented online.

Far from being what outsiders may see as a teen sensation, the principles of using social networking technology have been with us since Sir Tim Berners-Lee wrote a proposal for information management back in 1990 (the internet as we know it today). In fact, the idea of sharing and collaborating on information online goes back to the 1950s, when first the military and then the universities started to network information.

For a very long time before web-savvy teenagers got their hands on these social tools, the more technical and scientific amongst us used online networks to email each other, to share information and to collaborate online. Some of these enthusiasts may have even organised meetings using this technology!

By the mid 1990s we had Amazon.com online, and we were starting to see an internet that even non-techie people could use. We started to see people contributing to bulletin boards for the first time in large numbers, as technology made the action simpler. Very soon after this period we started to see the type of social network sites that we are more familiar with today: those that allow us to find and connect with old friends. Today social networking sites and social media technology allow even the semi-computer-literate amongst us to build networks of connections, to talk to them and to find useful information through our expanded network of 'friends'.

For the uninitiated, then, online social technology may seem a totally new concept and in some cases may appear quite dumbfounding. However, in reality it is just an extension of what we do in real life – and that is what schools have to understand. Just as in real life you visit a school to get a 'feel' for it, so we can now provide this information online, to a larger audience and conveying much wider and deeper information. We can film teachers, sports clubs, classes, lectures, field trips, and (well, let's be honest) anything that portrays an honest, positive and 'on-brand' attitude from the school.

This is just for starters. Why? Because online social technology allows you to do so much more than was once possible. Schools can now create their own online communities and provide potential customers with engaging information that satisfies exactly what they want and expect from a school. You have a choice of audience: teachers, pupils, parents and the alumni. By understanding your audience you are able to create a campaign aimed specifically at its members. By contrast, we too often make the mistake of using a scatter-gun approach, vainly hoping that one single social media campaign can satisfy all audiences.

The real beauty of modern online social tools lies in the fact that, unlike traditional advertising, this form of marketing is no longer a one-way broadcast approach. Online social media technology allows us to ask questions and lets our audience talk back to us. This dialogue approach allows us to learn so much from those who constitute our market, providing information that can be used to make decisions on how you market or even operate as a school in the future. Think of it as continuous market research.

There is a large collection of sites that can help you create communities and communicate better with your audiences. You give information in so many ways, including the written word, video, podcasts and photos. What has to be established is that by using social media to market your school you are not using such opportunities as a direct and overt advertising tool. Your campaign is to communicate, help, listen and solve problems if required. It is not a tool to hard-sell – but it can be a vital support to the process.

Online social networks are very viral in nature and some of the fastest growing businesses in the United States have used this 'word of mouth', nature to great effect – rather in the same way that when we feel positive about a service or product, we tell people about it.

Nowadays this process happens online without us having to prompt it – and to a much larger audience. The testimonials that social networking contains are a great source of information for any prospective pupil or parent; they can provide a conclusively positive response to the age-old question: 'Do I trust the school to provide an excellent education and life skills?'

This brings us to a really excellent and important aspect of online social technology and networks. More and more of a school's prospective families are paying less attention to its marketing material, because they know that it has been written by someone who has been paid to say good things about the school. As a group of online consumers and information gatherers, people now want impartial, honest, transparent information with no spin. They are looking to 'people like ourselves' to give us 'real' information and advice. Social networking allows them to acquire it.

Social media allow anyone to write down their thoughts about a product and service, and then they allow our potential customers to search for this information. Whether you like this or not *your* school is being talked about – mostly in a positive light, although sometimes there could be less positive information out there as well. By being a part of these conversations and inviting people on to your network, you can start to control this information a little better and you can counter any negative comments as they arise.

We now have a huge population of digital natives (those who have been born into the digital age, and who never knew what the world was like before it existed). They are people who do not use, and who are totally uninfluenced by, traditional marketing and advertising techniques. These are people who use only the internet to find out their information and who are more and more influenced by social networks, social technology and the engaging information contained within.

Online social media technologies and networking are not going away!

Chapter 5

The marketing and admissions department: an overview

Janet Smith

An efficient and effective marketing and admissions function within educational institutions is fundamental to their survival and continued success. Why? Because securing business is crucial during a time of turbulence in the economy and of political change. Add to this situation the increasingly selective, smaller customer base and highly competitive marketplace described in the 2010 ISC census, and the need for any school to compete successfully within its market becomes all too clear.

Schools that are proactive and that market well, drawing from across the marketing mix and employing proactive strategies, will thrive, while those that are slow to respond, inflexible or unclear about their direction, will struggle. Having an integrated, professional and customer-focused marketing and admissions operation gives a school an important competitive advantage.

The Chartered Institute of Marketing (CIM) describes marketing as:

> ...the process by which companies determine what products or services may be of interest to customers, and the strategy to use in sales, communications and business development.

Simplified and applied to a school setting, this can be rendered as:

> ...the process by which schools determine what educational provision may be of interest to parents and children, and the recruitment and retention strategies to use.

Unlike multinational companies, in a school environment the admissions staff – if they exist – do not simply equate to the sales force, although there are of course certain similarities.

This chapter considers a number of practical issues about marketing and admissions. It aims to include organisational issues such as personnel; lines of reporting and accountability; information management; budgeting and communication. However, in many schools these will also touch closely on the development or foundation function, involved in fundraising and alumni management. What a chapter such as this cannot do is to prescribe the exact make-up of the marketing and admissions 'team' or 'department', because that is the prerogative of each school and is dependent upon individual circumstances.

The way in which pupils are recruited and admitted varies greatly throughout the independent sector. It depends on factors such as the evolution and culture of each school; its type and size; the understanding of the organisation as a business; the available budget and the experience and preferences of the leadership team.

In some institutions – for example small preparatory schools – staff may be employed part-time or only during term time. They may multi-task, combining marketing and admissions work with other roles: such people may include the Head's secretary, those involved in teaching and house duties and/or in development/fundraising and enterprise management.

At the other end of the scale of size, very large boarding schools may have an international recruitment department allied to the admissions office. Those schools that are members of chains controlled by wholly independent providers may have individual school admissions and marketing staff who report not only to the school's Head but also to a specialist head of marketing for the group as a whole.

In 2009 an online school marketing survey of a cross-section of 200 independent schools was conducted by a well-established company that specialises in providing a range of services to the sector. The survey revealed that a quarter of schools, mostly operating at the senior age-range, have an 'integrated marketing and admissions department'. About a third of the preparatory schools surveyed had one person handling marketing and admissions alone. In 39% of the schools there was a full-time member of staff responsible for marketing.

However, a somewhat perturbing result showed that: '...one school in ten, even in today's highly competitive environment, has no member of staff [specifically] responsible for marketing.' It goes without saying, of course, that every member of staff has, or should have, a broad responsibility for marketing the school – seizing every opportunity to attract new entrants and to enhance its reputation, thereby protecting their own interests as well – but in practical terms the majority of schools feel that, ideally, a specific individual should hold the specialist brief.

The experience and background of staff varies widely. The survey confirmed that a growing number of school marketers (62%) possess either a relevant professional qualification – usually Chartered Institute of Marketing (CIM) – or some previous marketing experience. However, some staff come directly into marketing schools from other disciplines and occupations.

Recruiting, recognising and retaining the right kind of staff from outside or inside the organisation, who are concerned in any way with admissions and marketing, is extremely important. In sales terms, the 'product' that an independent school 'sells' is potentially life changing: it is certainly at the high-value end of the market, worth literally thousands of pounds! Now, what kind of sales person is required for that sort of transaction?

All too often the professional development needs of administrative staff are overlooked. To whom can one turn for advice and guidance? The flagship professional organisation of school marketers is unquestionably the Association of Marketing and Development in Independent Schools (AMDIS). AMDIS is a highly regarded and very active professional body, which has been in existence since the early 1990s, offering courses and qualifications in marketing. AMDIS is currently in discussion with the CIM to gain recognition as an accredited provider of professional development courses and events.

More recently, AMDIS has introduced a qualification for admissions staff to meet their specialised training and development needs, and this qualification includes elements of marketing. Other organisations (for example, the ISC) hold one-day seminars on topical issues. However, as well as attending seminars, much can be gained by staff simply meeting with their opposite numbers in other schools. In the independent sector at all levels, other schools are our rivals, but our opposite numbers can also be our friends, and networking brings its own rewards: the senior management should encourage marketing staff to look outside and beyond their own organisation to find out what is happening right across the market, to gain ideas and to regenerate themselves.

The admissions and marketing team – and they *must* operate as a team – distil and disseminate the Head's vision and ethos of the school. From this strategic vision flow the school development plan and all other initiatives, including the marketing plan with its strategic priorities and targets. These should be absorbed and interpreted by all the staff and translated into tactical and tangible actions with outcomes that are monitored, assessed and adjusted through regular review and discussion by the senior management team, and reported to the governors.

In larger schools, locating the marketing and admissions team within the same office has mutual benefits: there will be opportunities for mentoring; sharing information; supporting campaigns; assisting with events; tutoring with information technology systems; giving hands-on help with large-scale tasks; covering during brief absences where possible and, where necessary, standing-in for one's colleagues.

This 'nerve-centre' of the school should not work in isolation. Sharing, or being in close proximity to, other offices or departments (such as the bursary or general office) can be advantageous to the organisation as a whole. This is particularly beneficial, for example, in providing holiday cover so that the operation is never allowed to grind to a halt.

In terms of lines of reporting, the person heading up the admissions team – the registrar or admissions manager, whatever his/her title – and the person responsible for marketing may report direct to the Head. However in some, mostly larger, schools another senior member of staff may carry the overall responsibility for external communications (marketing, admissions, development) and will represent the interests, activities and concerns of these operational areas to the leadership team as a whole, updating it with information on a regular basis.

Whereas the 'pure' marketer may or may not have regular meetings with the Head, it is more often the practice for the registrar (a different title with a different emphasis) to have frequent and direct contact with the Head – especially when decisions are being made about offering places. Their relationship must be one of synergy, built on professional trust and respect, in which advice is given and taken and opinions are expressed openly between both parties. Both will take into account many diverse factors when considering individual admission cases, or specific changes in the market, which have a bearing on admissions policy and practice.

A good registrar will learn to know in advance, by experience and instinct, what the Head's decision is likely to be in the majority of cases; s/he will not waste the Head's valuable time by presenting cases that have no hope of being offered a place, for whatever reason.

The registrar is unique in that s/he sees and operates in both directions – outwards, reaping the efforts of marketing, and inwards, processing the applications through to arrival and sometimes beyond. Like the marketer, the registrar becomes aware of the trends in the market and will track changes in the pattern and volume of demand, as well as (in a boarding school) monitoring the value of business generated by international agents. The registrar is also in a special position, in the sense of having had contact with every family and pupil in the school; s/he is the first point of contact between home and school and, no matter how much of a cliché it is, first impressions most definitely *do* count.

At a time when more families are first-time buyers, a sensitive and approachable registrar can interpret the new and sometimes confusing experience of independent education to 'freshers' in a logical, reassuring and non-patronising way. Admissions staff must excel in organisational and customer care skills and be able to remain calm, polite and cheerful, even in the face of brusque or confrontational phone calls. Theirs is an oft-times pressurised environment, coping with the demands of increasingly discerning – and sometimes discourteous – parents and other external constituents from one side, while responding to the needs and constraints of the school on the other.

Teamwork is at the centre of an efficient and effective marketing and admissions operation, and its *modus operandi* is comparable to a relay race. At its most basic, the function of the marketer is a continuous and continual process of attracting the attention of the identified target markets, making potential customers aware of the school's existence and provision. Having raised interest and stimulated the target market, enquiries are channelled to the admissions staff to continue the marketing process through to completion, thereby 'clinching the deal'.

Once this has occurred, and the family joins the school, the admissions team hands over the precious cargo to other staff and generally moves on to the next generation of would-be applicants. The process of recruitment does not occur singly or in isolation: the admissions team may be dealing with dozens, if not hundreds, of cases at varying stages of the recruitment journey. The end-results of the marketer's work are intangible and may go unrecognised, whereas the results of the admissions staff are very tangible: new pupils.

Internal communication across the school is as important as external communication with those seeking a school. This is something to be kept under review, especially in some large boarding schools where the admissions process is decentralised as a result of individual houseparents keeping in contact with prospective parents and operating their own, house-based, admissions lists.

Here there is a risk of misunderstandings between houses and the admissions office, especially if records are being kept manually. Should the family links not be maintained or the admissions office not be aware of a family's interest, the school may risk losing potential customers and, more importantly, vital revenue and (possibly) reputation. There is a further risk, too: that a school may overestimate the numbers of families still interested in places, because families who registered long ago but have now decided to go elsewhere have not been identified.

Thus the recording and tracking of enquiries, visitors, registrations, and even withdrawals, is at the heart of the admissions function, whether it be centralised or decentralised. Having a fail-safe management information system (MIS) is essential for admissions staff and marketers.

Providing such systems for schools is an important and growing business, both for providers and schools. Most schools have well-developed and sophisticated means for gathering and reporting information, using their databases and IT packages. Larger senior schools may have a member of staff responsible for MIS, usually within the IT department; smaller schools will rely on training sessions and online or telephone help from their MIS providers.

While all schools would ideally like to acquire one unified system to meet all the needs across the school's diverse functions – marketing, admissions, academic reporting, accounts, alumni relations, *etc* – I have yet to hear of a school having one integrated, robust MIS system, or a single system that completely satisfies all requirements. This is an area where compromises have to be made, and often systems that are successful in one part of the school's operation seem to be weak in another.

However, the recording and extracting of management information, which is important for the marketer, is a requirement that should not be overlooked. Without being able to track information and/or provide meaningful statistics, how can the marketer gauge the effectiveness and return of investment on, for example, a new website or advertising campaign, or assess how parents have heard about the school? More work needs to be done by IT specialists and database providers in this area, so that schools can ensure that they meet their customers' needs.

Meanwhile, no matter which system is used, great care needs to be taken when inputting data and extracting information. It is unreasonable to expect a system to produce meaningful reports when the information has been entered incorrectly – for example by selecting the wrong destination 'field' or by not using the fields at all. Consideration needs to be given to the design of registration and other forms that capture fundamental customer information.

A little forethought about the sections to be completed by parents will assist greatly when the information is later entered into fields on the database and still later manipulated to produce management reports. For example, why ask the religion of the pupil on the registration form if this information (which is required by the ISC census for pupils actually on the roll) is not essential until the later stages of recruitment? Not only that, but admissions departments also need to be mindful of the requirement to dispense with data that can be of no further use. Culling the records of enquirers or others who are well past the upper entry age of the school on a cyclical basis is not only good practice and required under data protection law, but will also free up valuable space on the database.

While the admissions staff will use the full range of pupil management functions that their database provides, the marketer will probably concentrate on the records within the 'other schools' section, showing those organisations from which pupils come. Where preparatory schools are concerned, this includes nurseries, pre-preps and future schools; for senior schools, it may involve state junior and independent preparatory feeder schools – together with information about those international schools where a boarding school is recruiting from overseas.

The importance of cultivating these key sources of future clients cannot be over emphasised, and building and maintaining accurate records is essential. Developing the relationship between one's own school and its feeder schools is a key aspect of the public relations function of the marketing and admissions team. Understanding feeder schools as a target group, not as one mass but in terms of their individual Heads, staff, children and parents, and creating attractive activities and opportunities for each of these targets, is central to building fruitful relationships.

Senior school staff should remember that all one's competitor schools will also be courting the same feeder preparatory and primary schools. Senior schools must never assume that preparatory schools are less busy than they are, or are by definition less well resourced or lacking in marketing acumen.

Heads and specialist staff should be prepared to visit their feeder institutions as well as to host individual Heads' visits and group gatherings. Special relationships need to be fostered with maintained primary feeder schools, which operate in a completely different environment to independent schools. The Charities' Act has probably afforded schools an even greater incentive for more creative thinking in this area: some larger schools have created outreach posts with this in mind.

Allocating sufficient funds for marketing activity is an important consideration for governors, guided by the Head, who relies in turn on the experience and forward planning ability of the manager concerned. Although the aim is to ensure that everyone is responsible for marketing the school, not *all* expenditure can be attributed to the marketing department! But how much is enough when it comes to budget allocation?

The survey already quoted found that the average spend on marketing activities (excluding salaries) was about 1.1% of fee turnover. How each school spends its budget varies, but typically it includes promotional materials and media such as the prospectus, newsletters and advertising. More frequently nowadays, schools are using electronic communication channels including websites, e-newsletters and social media to reach their customers.

It is imperative that during a time of restricted spending individuals monitor, control and spend their budget prudently. It is a wise and brave governing body that defends, and does not reduce, the marketing budget during a recession, as the latter course would be self defeating and could potentially place the school in a vulnerable position, both in the short and longer term. However, marketing should not be the school's spendthrift department!

Personal recommendation by current customers is most often cited as the source of generating new custom for all businesses – and schools are no exception to this rule. Internal marketing to current parents by seeking their views, listening to and communicating with them, and ensuring that they and their children feel valued and are satisfied, is critically important in ensuring ongoing success.

In recent years the need to raise funds for bursaries, current projects, the enhancement of existing facilities and the creation of future developments, has seen the introduction of 'development' or 'foundation' initiatives. To use a marketing concept itself, marketing has become a mature product in schools, and there is a growing trend in senior schools to combine the roles of marketing and development, particularly at management or senior management level. Indeed, often the all-round importance of the job and the expectations connected with it are reflected in the attractive remuneration packages offered to candidates.

So, how desirable is it to have a unified management structure for marketing and development? Co-locating admissions and marketing staff (as mentioned earlier) may make sense, but there are pros and cons of combining departments and including the development staff in the same office. Obviously practical constraints, such as the size and layout of the school buildings, have to be taken into consideration.

The main arguments in favour of such an approach are that admissions, marketing and development are all business functions and can share expertise across the areas, such as with brochure production; they can support and assist each other, particularly at times of pressure during a marketing or development campaign; communications may be improved; potential donor families can be identified early.

The counter-arguments may be that an imbalance is perceived or actually present in the resources (usually staffing or budget) in one area or the other; resentment may arise over the role or importance given to that area, and although both admissions and development staff are largely creating with tangible results, the development office tends to do it over a longer time-scale.

Whatever decision a school takes, in both areas some issues of a confidential nature will be discussed, such as applications for financial assistance or the need for learning support (admissions) or a legacy or large donation (development) from a constituent who wishes to remain anonymous. All staff working in combined roles and work-spaces are called upon to show absolute professionalism and confidentiality at all times.

Ultimately, each school must decide for itself what works best, and the size of a school may well be the determining factor in the final decision, with smaller schools opting for a combined structure. Yet size and scale of numbers and budget are not the only determinants: many of the skills required by school marketers and development staff are common to both areas and therefore transferable, even if there is a difference in the remit of each function within the organisation.

Essentially, without marketing attracting the right type of customers, and admissions recruiting the right balance and numbers, there would be few opportunities for development to cultivate new supporter-constituencies within the school body. Thus marketing continues to hold its place alongside development – and the two functions can be mutually sustaining. Whatever the structural outcomes, all three areas of marketing, admissions and development are concerned with customer service. Whether there is one person or a team of ten involved, in these customer-facing roles everyone needs to be passionate about their work and to contribute to the current and future standing of the business.

Finally, as a team, the admissions and marketing staff should share successes from within and be encouraged by those to whom they report. There is always room for improvement and none for complacency. Many departments welcome 'mystery shoppers' and customer feedback, and they are continually seeking ways to improve their service.

Admissions and marketing staff should be afforded due regard in the school for their key function in securing new customers for the business – and pupils for the classroom. Recognition of a job well done is always appreciated: cultivating a praise culture within schools is not just the prerogative of pupils! By motivating and empowering the marketing and admissions team – and other staff – to perform well and to meet targets, the school will prosper, and will continue to enjoy celebrating its well earned, collective success now and for the future.

Chapter 6

Market research and strategic planning

Dick Davison

The most famous axiom about marketing, variously attributed to Lord Leverhulme and Henry Ford amongst others, and usually quoted by those who instinctively mistrust the theory and practice of marketing, is the one that goes: "I know that half the money we spend on advertising is wasted. The trouble is, I don't know which half."

My own view is that much more than half the modest amount spent by most schools on advertising is demonstrably wasted. That fact alone should make any decision to carry out market research rather easier to justify. But the dilemma remains, and it applies to most marketing activities – for schools, as for all businesses: how do we know who we are trying to address and how do we identify the most effective means of addressing them? No marketing strategy that ignores these fundamental questions is worth the effort of producing it. Therein lies the importance of research.

Can you define your school's market? Do you know the extent of your catchment area? Do you know what are the socio-demographic characteristics of your current parents? Where do you find more such families? What newspapers do they read and how do they behave as consumers? What do they think of your school? What words do they use to describe it? What do the Heads of feeder schools know about your school, and what do they tell parents? Why do parents who consider but reject your school act as they do? How much do parents rely on digital communications to find out about schools? What influences sixth-formers to stay on at your school after GCSE – or to go elsewhere? What do parents think of your competitors? And just how far and how deep is their reach into your recruitment area?

The answers to these and many similar questions will form the foundation of a secure marketing strategy for your school. Let's set out some of the ways in which these answers can be found and why they are important.

Researching your market

Once upon a time, school marketing was based around a big map in the registrar's office, with a colourful forest of display pins marking the addresses of all current pupils. An excellent start, but times have moved on. Using the same raw materials – *ie* pupils' addresses – we can now analyse the school's market in much greater detail.

A socio-demographic analysis will take your pupils' postcodes and, using commercial databases, will classify their families into the 50-odd categories devised by social research companies to define the way people live and how they spend their time and money.

These categories are given colourful – and sometimes misleading – titles: 'affluent greys'; 'prosperous professionals'; 'secure families'. Derived from census data and numerous other databases (every transaction involving digital transfer of money, for example, is stored and analysed in a database somewhere), these categories give a surprisingly precise definition of the way people behave as consumers. Mapping their addresses gives a very reliable guide to the neighbourhoods in which they tend to cluster.

So analysis of your current pupil profile and applying it to your catchment area will allow you to see where the greatest concentrations of similar families are actually situated. The chances are that the majority of the families will appear in one of only about half-a-dozen classifications towards the top of the socio-demographic scale.

What will this permit you to do? At its simplest, it will show you whether you are exploiting the full potential of your market, or where there are areas of apparent high potential in which you are not recruiting. It will help you plan your transport provision – ensuring that you serve the areas of greatest potential – or to extend your transport reach as an incentive to parents. It will show you where to target most effectively your marketing initiatives: leaflet distribution; recruitment roadshows; initiatives for feeder schools and the like.

More sophisticated analyses will show you whether the child population in your target areas is expected to rise or fall, or to plot the effect of the recruitment activities of your competitors on your own catchment area. They can also help you to promote your school's bursary provision: just as a socio-demographic analysis can accurately describe the location of the families that are *most* able to afford your fees, so it can show where to find those *least* able to do so. And it's a simple matter from there to identifying likely primary schools, for example, or supermarkets, medical centres and libraries where you could distribute your bursary flyer.

Researching your parents
The other hackneyed axiom about school marketing is that 'it's all word of mouth'. This one, at least, is largely true. What isn't true, however, is that you can't do anything about WOM reputation – a big subject in itself beyond the scope of this article. The first thing you can, and must, do is to find out as much as you can about what parents actually think and say.

The conventional and most often used method of researching parental opinion is the questionnaire. In the past, this was generally a paper form, completed in hard copy with the results painstakingly collated and analysed. This exercise, too, has gone digital – with enormous gains in levels of response, ease of analysis and, of course, economy. A survey of parental opinion, conducted on a secure web page, will yield a response rate typically in the 35-55% range; using relatively simple software, it can be conveniently analysed and cross-tabulated (to allow you, for example, to contrast the views of newly-arrived families with those of longer standing).

A word of warning: some schools are tempted to rely on the surveys conducted by school inspectors during the inspection process. For marketing purposes, these may be helpful, but they are only part of the story. Inspectors are concerned to find out about things like the appropriate balance between curricular and co-curricular activities, the quality of academic and careers advice and the handling of concerns and complaints: they have little or no interest in how parents found out about the school; what they think of the prospectus and the website; whether they think the school offers value for money; what words they use to describe it to others; what alternative schools they considered and what they think of them.

It is particularly important to find out what factors especially influenced parents in choosing the school: class size; single-sex/coeducation; academic results; cultural opportunities; sports; quality of teaching – and how they rate the school's performance on these same factors. Cross-referencing those responses will give you an infallible fix on the priorities for action so far as parents are concerned.

One especially revealing exercise is to ask parents to choose, from a spectrum of epithets, the three they would be most likely to choose to describe the school. The 'spider chart' resulting from their responses can tell you more about your school's distinctive offer to the market than almost anything else. The chart below shows the results from a coeducational day school that achieves the rare distinction of being most likely to be described as 'welcoming' and 'friendly' as well as 'academic'.

But the questionnaire will only go so far. The constraints of a survey form that can be easily and quickly completed, and just as easily analysed,

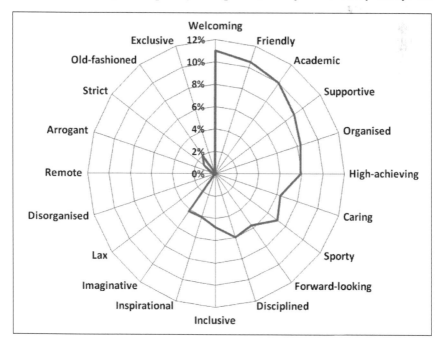

inevitably reduce specifics to generalities. There may be vital issues that you want to unpick in greater detail: just what difference has a rival school's change to coeducation made; how unsettled have parents been by a change of Head; how would they like to see the school develop in future?

To get a better idea of how parents' reactions colour their choices, and what they say to others, you need to employ more qualitative means of research: one-to-one telephone interviews, or focus groups. For these, as for much else in focusing your marketing effort, you may have to turn to outside help. Not only do focus groups require skilled and sensitive handling, but parents are in general much more likely to give their views candidly to a disinterested third party under controlled conditions of individual confidentiality.

Parents who decide not to join you: finding out why not

Just as important as the opinions of current parents, perhaps even more so, is discovering why those parents who made an enquiry, visited you, maybe even were offered a place but failed to find your school irresistible. You may *think* you know why; you may even be tempted to believe that the reasons are mostly financial but, in truth, you won't *know* this for certain until you have researched their views objectively. These so-called 'decliner interviews' are a vital source of information, not only about how your own school is perceived but about your competitors too.

Contrary to a widely-held view, parents do not mind being asked these things. In fact, most positively relish the opportunity to talk about their choice and the reasons for it. But, as with current parents, the problem is getting past natural courtesy and the reluctance to offend, and it will almost certainly yield more reliable results if you use an experienced external interviewer – having first warned parents that you are conducting the research and given them the opportunity to decline to take part. In practice, few do so.

To see ourselves as others see us

Two other pieces of research will help to locate where your school stands in public estimation, and particularly in the estimation of those who might consider it for their children.

The Heads of feeder schools – prep and primary schools, if yours is a senior school; pre-preps and nurseries if a junior or prep school – are key opinion-formers. Parents often ask for their advice and they often give it unasked. Do they know what your school is like now, or are they relying on second-hand or out-of-date information? Schools are often surprised, even alarmed, by the entrenched or inaccurate views held by these influential customer-brokers. Telephone interviews, again conducted by commissioned third-party researchers, are invariably revealing.

Don't forget, too, the value of the mystery shopper – the arranged visit by an incognito researcher, playing the part of a prospective parent – to report on the effectiveness and approachability of your admissions staff; the quality of your prospectus and website; accessibility and signage; first impressions; the structure and friendliness of the tour; the usefulness and comprehensiveness of information provided; the efficacy of follow-up activities. And why not get your competitors mystery-shopped too, by the same agent and to the same objective criteria?

Data capture

It is a mistake to think of research as something that is conducted only in substantial one-off projects. A vital element of the evidence base for a marketing strategy is the information you can gather every day (especially from prospective parents), and then process and analyse regularly. Every school collects basic information from enquirers: names, contact details, date of birth and other information about the child; date of possible entry to the school; how they found out about the school, and so on. Fewer schools, perhaps, collect similar information from parents who come to open days or open evenings.

Even fewer schools make full use of this vital information once they have acquired it. As a result, they are able neither to track the progress of individual enquiries through the admissions process, nor to analyse and report on trends. Having all available information at your fingertips for every subsequent contact, whether it is a visit or another call for information, is vital to good contact management. It is equally important to be able to keep track of your success in steering initial contacts through to admission.

Very few schools have any idea what their 'funnel ratio' is (*ie* the ratio of enquiries to visits; to registrations; to admissions), let alone whether it is getting better or worse. Too many schools have no idea what happens to enquirers who are in touch only once, perhaps to ask for a prospectus. In any sales-oriented business, all such contacts are treated like precious ore, and are handled and recorded just as carefully.

It's not a good idea to try to do any of this using manually-maintained paper records. Digital technology makes it all much easier and there are a number of bespoke admissions software packages, some of them integrated with standard school management information systems.

The strategic marketing plan

The evidence gathered by using the forms of research described above will equip you with most of the information you need to prepare a coherent strategic marketing plan. You may wish to involve a number of people in this process: your marketing director or manager and your registrar, of course, but also other members of the senior team; governors (especially those with relevant expertise), and other members of the teaching and non-teaching staff whose responsibilities bring them in close and regular contact with parents.

It is helpful to structure a strategic plan along the following lines:

a) *Key issues.* Research should help you to identify what the key issues are, which your strategy should address. You may find that your school has an unjustified reputation for being a hothouse or exam-factory; that your marketing collateral – website, prospectus, advertisements, *etc* – is seen as out-of-date or inappropriate to your school's high-quality brand; that your external communications with the community and the media are poorly developed, or that your internal marketing and admissions functions are poorly co-ordinated, staffed and resourced. These key issues should be identified and set out in priority order.

b) *Marketing objectives.* In similar order of priority, the strategy should set out clearly the objectives it aims to fulfil: *eg* to create a marketing and admissions capability in line with best practice in the sector; to improve internal and external communications; to compete more effectively with neighbouring schools; to strengthen the school's brand identity; to increase recruitment at Years 7 or 9; to increase the recruitment of UK boarders; to improve recruitment and retention to the sixth form. The objectives will dictate the next section.

c) *Marketing strategies.* This section will set out the long-term (three- or five-year) strategies to deliver the objectives: staffing changes and new appointments; how internal and external communications are going to be improved; priority areas for the enhancement of recruiting; a review of marketing publications and the commissioning of their replacements; greater use of digital technologies; e-marketing and social networking sites; strategies for increasing the recruitment potential of your sixth form.

d) *Actions, targets and monitoring.* The first year's actions in pursuit of the strategic goals need to be set out clearly, with a timetable for implementation, a clear identification of responsibility for members of staff and a target outcome. What will success look like for each of the actions? It should go without saying that the strategy and action plan should be kept under regular review.

Not the least advantage of a structured plan of this kind is that it will help to take the unplanned and largely reactive element out of your school's advertising. Advertising will be planned around specific events; its cost will be structured into the budget and its effectiveness monitored. You may not be able to answer Lord Leverhulme's dilemma with absolute precision, but you will have a clear answer to the governor or parent who wonders why you haven't advertised in *Borsetshire Life* when 'everyone else was there'.

Don't forget, in all this, the rest of your staff. In too many schools, teachers regard marketing as being none of their responsibility: "I'm here to teach – it's the Head's/marketing manager's job to make sure there are enough pupils to teach." This is an all-too common attitude that ignores the critically important contribution that every member of staff makes to the marketing effort – from the language used in individual pupil reports to the tone of voice that the receptionist adopts with exasperating parents. If staff have had some involvement in the preparation of the marketing plan, and if they are given a clear idea of how they can contribute to its success (or conversely to undermine it), it is much more likely to achieve the objectives you set.

Using consultants

How much of this can a school do for itself? You would expect a consultant to say how important it is to have an expert to deliver your research and to assist your planning. Some of the more complex socio-demographic research techniques certainly require external expertise, and the value of a third party in getting candid views from parents and others has already been explained. Yet in truth, much of what I've described lies within the competence of many, if not most, schools.

In marketing above all, however, it is invaluable to have an external perspective. It is too easy to imagine you know how the school is perceived; to believe that your website is attractive, user-friendly and effective; to think that, because your registrar has done a good job for years, all is well. You may find yourself unsurprised by much of what a consultant or external researcher tells you – although in my experience most schools are taken unawares either by some finding or by the relative importance of a particular factor. And you will at least have the security of knowing that your plans are based on verifiable evidence, objectively gathered, and that they have been measured against the best practice in the sector.

Chapter 7

Branding and key messages

Katherine Bolton

A *brand* is what gives any organisation its identity in the minds of both its potential and its existing customers. The former need to be given a sense of *brand awareness*: the latter should have a fulfilling *brand experience*.

Wikipedia defines a 'brand image' as: 'A symbolic construct created within the minds of people and consist[ing] of all the information and expectations associated with a product or service.' Your brand helps you to give the impression that your organisation is very special – even unique. It is made up of many individual elements, including everything from a name, a logo, symbols and slogans, to the way your staff are dressed and the manner in which the phone is answered. If your *brand management* is good, making these component parts imaginative and consistent – they can be a very powerful marketing tool.

Branding is therefore a complex process that involves a significant investment of time and budget. As the foundation of a marketing strategy for any business, however, the end result is well worth the effort. The early cattle owners found that if they wanted to keep their cattle, branding them with a hot iron stamp was time well spent: branding of a different type is a similarly valuable tool for those of us marketing businesses in the modern age.

As a start, establish where you are now, compared to where you want to be. Does your marketing strategy need an injection of new ideas, or is your first step to write a strategy? Do you feel that your marketing is built on strong foundations, or do you need to go back to basics before embarking on ambitious marketing activities? Is the concept of a marketing department new to your school, or do you have a long tradition of marketing?

Whatever your situation, the fast-moving discipline of marketing always presents new challenges. Taking the time out to understand your

Unique Selling Propositions (USPs) and key messages, and to devise a fresh, cohesive approach can provide not only renewed inspiration and enthusiasm, but should also improve return on investment and results.

The process of defining your USPs is not always as straightforward as you may think. The reason is twofold: first, not all key stakeholders involved in the process may agree on the USPs (at least initially); and secondly, you may be faced with the circumstance whereby many of your competitors are offering, essentially, the same benefits to the same target market. But dig a little deeper and you will always be able to find your point of difference.

It is worth taking the time to look at your school to understand where the differences lie compared with your competitors: this will then help to underpin how the school will be marketed in the future. USPs can be defined as those features that provide specific and tangible benefits to your target market; that set you apart from your competitors. You might have exceptional sports facilities, a particular strength in music and drama, or outstanding academic results. Be ready to support your USPs with facts and figures as appropriate.

This is also a good time to review any changes you might want or need to make to the features – and therefore the benefits – you offer, in response to demand. For instance, would admissions to your nursery be much higher if you opened one hour earlier and closed one hour later? As well as an overarching USP for the school at large, you may well develop individual USPs for the different elements of the school – for instance the nursery, the junior school, the senior school and the sixth form.

Once you have your USPs agreed, it is time to turn to the development of your key messages to ensure that your USPs are clearly communicated to your current and prospective parents and pupils. But a word of caution here: don't close the book on your USPs completely at this point; they will naturally change over time, to take into account not only changes in the business environment and your target market, but also the evolution of the benefits that you and your competitors offer.

Additionally, when developing your USPs and key messages, be careful not to rush to rigid and inflexible assumptions. Be open to different views and new ideas from key stakeholders and current pupils. If budgets allow, undertake some market research in the form of focus groups or surveys, both of current and prospective parents, to establish what they think of the school (the good, the bad and the ugly features) and also, critically, what they look for in a school. Ask why, in the case of prospective parents, they might be deciding to send their children elsewhere.

The next step is to define your key messages. As with your USPs, your key messages will inevitably change over time, so regular re-evaluation is essential to keep them fresh, along with your marketing activities and the interest of your target market.

Key messages are essentially the 'headlines' of your marketing campaigns. They are the pieces of information that you want people to remember and that inspire them to take action. They promote your USPs and express the benefits to your target market. Researching the key messages of your competitors, before making a final decision about your own, will ensure there are no embarrassing overlaps or similarities. However, don't do this too early in the process: it is helpful not to seek out the key messages of your competitors when initially drafting yours, so that you are not subconsciously influenced by what your rivals are saying about themselves.

Once you have defined your USPs and key messages, they form the building blocks from which the physical brand is built. So you will then need to create a brand, and brand guidelines.

Your brand is not just your logo, or your school crest – although this is a good place to start in building solid foundations for marketing. Important questions to ask at this early stage are:

- Is the logo clear, attractive, up-to-date and in tune with the school's present culture and strengths, whilst still reflecting its history?
- Is it instantly recognisable and able to stand out against your competitors for all the right reasons?
- Is it accompanied by an understanding among key staff of how the 'logo' becomes a 'brand' through consistent roll-out on everything from letterhead to livery, as set out in your brand guidelines?

If the answer to most to these questions is 'no', you have probably concluded that your logo leaves something to be desired and that the development of the school's brand is still very much work in progress. Fear not; this is not an uncommon situation and it is far better to recognise it now and address it head on.

If this is indeed the case, avoid the temptation to refresh the logo in-house, unless you are lucky enough to have an experienced creative team at your disposal. Instead, employ the services of a design agency that can help you achieve the very best result and, ultimately, to maximise return on investment. Work closely with it to ensure it understands the ethos, values, history, direction and target market of the school, as well as who your main competitors are – and, of course, your current USPs and key messages.

Involve key stakeholders in the decision-making process when it comes to deciding on the visual identity. Your Head, deputy head, marketing and admissions teams, bursar, registrar, governors, and parent and pupil body groups will all provide valuable input. However, be prepared for some people to be less than enthusiastic at the idea of change: it is not something everyone embraces, nor can you please all parties. While involving these groups at an early stage can help enormously, the final decision should be made by a select group of your choice.

Once the logo has been selected, you can move to the natural next step: developing a clear set of brand guidelines that lays out a suite of agreed uses of the logo (how it will appear in colour, black and white, *etc*), fonts, colours and document templates. Brand guidelines should also help to establish a tone of voice for the school, by employing tactics such as agreed standard sign offs to emails and letters (but more on that later when we consider brand management and marketing implementation). Empower appropriate members of the team with the knowledge and importance of these brand guidelines; the process of adhering to them will be made easier.

Once you have a strong logo and brand guidelines, assume the role of brand guardian so that you can have the confidence that all your marketing collateral will be on-target, on-message and representative of the school, and also will be true to your USPs and key messages. Ideally, you should then continue to act as the point of final sign off for all marketing collateral.

The next stage is marketing planning and goal setting. Now that you have taken stock of the USPs and key messages, and have used these to develop the school brand, it is time to ensure these are dovetailed within your implementation. It is surprisingly common for businesses of all sizes not to have a marketing plan, or at least not one that is being implemented. Schools are included in this: often they have the intention and the skill, but they lack the time as the 'reactive' overtakes the 'proactive'. In other words, you may have a masterpiece of marketing strategy under your belt, but you may have struggled to implement it in quite the way you had intended.

Something not always understood is that marketing as a discipline encompasses a huge remit of responsibilities and areas of concern. So, unless you have a big team, you won't be able to implement all of the ideas addressed in your marketing strategy immediately. But don't get disheartened; fight back with a plan of attack!

Having a planning calendar is a simple but very effective tool. My own company uses this for all business types, including schools: it works well in mapping out a clear way forward that breaks down the mammoth discipline of marketing into manageable chunks. Your planning calendar can be as simple as an Excel spreadsheet with the months and weeks of the year in one column and the activities in the next.

Some activities will be very frequent and routine (daily website updates, weekly press releases); some will be monthly (article submission and parent newsletter); others will be annual, bi-annual or five year activities (prospectus design and print, review school signage and livery, *etc*).

In essence, review your marketing strategy; define your key priorities; draw up your planning calendar, then implement. Earmarking key campaign and other pre-set deadlines within your planning calendar enables you then to work back, to ensure that activities can be completed in time and that those dreaded last-minute rush jobs are few and far between.

Essentially, now that you have defined your USPs, key messages and the brand, you will want to ensure they are applied consistently through all marketing collateral. Brand management requires the control of many elements in the life of a brand, including those covered above, and also the implementation of marketing itself. Key elements of the marketing mix warrant particular attention: those discussed below form a list of things to include in your planning calendar. It is by no means exhaustive, but it should provide a useful reminder of those elements that are a priority.

First, stationery and templates: the grass roots of brand management. Consider all external (and if you can, internal) resources that are so routine that they can go unnoticed. These include letterhead, compliment slips, business cards, folders, word processing templates and email footers.

Secondly, the prospectus 'package'. First impressions count for a lot, and your prospectus will sit against those of your competitors on the coffee tables of prospective parents: it will be discussed at dinner parties along, of course, with personal experiences about the school.

Consider everything you need to send out to prospective parents and design it as the 'package' it is. This might include the covering letter, prospectus, fee guide, admissions form, and a folder, wallet, branded box or belly band to house all of these items. Don't stop there: think also about the envelope, address label and franking label, and think about where you could appropriately include your logo and key messages. Attention to detail counts for a lot: don't be afraid to be different, as these factors will drive conversations amongst prospective parents and pupils.

Thirdly, website and online marketing. In all likelihood, prospective parents will have already reviewed your website before they receive the prospectus package. But if not, they will almost inevitably look at it later on several occasions. The pace of change in the field of website development and online marketing is something remarkable to behold, so it pays to keep regular review in mind. But embrace this change: it is exciting and has potentially huge benefits to bring to your marketing.

Websites are a 'must-have'. They should not only be functionally brilliant, but also easy to navigate, optimised for search engines and filled with great copy. They also have as their overarching objective to *sell*: sell the school; the ethos; the grounds; the facility; the whole concept of the school. They must make it extremely easy for prospective parents to obtain the information they seek; you should consider providing answers to frequently asked questions and you must provide clear and prominently-displayed information about how to contact the school. Think about automating processes such as prospectus requests in the form of a Q & A page, or easy downloads of key information such as fees and term dates.

If you are unsure about whether your website is ticking all the right boxes in these respects, consider undertaking a usability testing exercise, to ensure that key users of the site can perform the fundamental actions and information requests with ease. Identify any points of frustration and failure and put them right. Prospective parents and pupils alike will be looking to get a feel of the school, and you won't have long to grab their attention.

Think outside the box, in terms of things that can set you apart: moving images; clips of school productions; video tours of the school; secure interactive areas where prospective pupils can take part in live chat with the head boy or girl; secure parent and former pupil information and networking areas.

Use your website as a communication tool – integrating website, email marketing, text message reminders and important announcements, and even e-commerce, as appropriate.

The website is of prime importance as a resource for current parents too: they need information on exam results, school closures, sports fixtures and term dates. The existence of a secure log-in area for parents allowed numerous schools to post work for pupils to complete at home during the snow closures in January 2010, demonstrating that websites can go beyond marketing and can assist in ensuring a smoother-running school.

As a marketing manager you will be keen to keep abreast of the latest trends in technology-driven marketing and social media, and to assess which of these are suitable and effective for marketing your particular school. Then you will need to set about capturing the advantages they offer – whether by setting up a Facebook page for sixth-formers to manage (under supervision, of course), by consideration of a viral marketing campaign, or by engaging key team members to write blogs.

Blogs are an increasingly useful tool to help parents and pupils to get a real feel for a prospective school. They also enable them to keep up-to-date with the latest news at their current school and, of course, to enable the schools themselves to retain strong, interested and informed parent and pupil alumni. Former pupils serve as an important set of ambassadors for your school. Blogs are also great for boosting your website's visibility on search engines, and can be linked with Twitter, LinkedIn and other social media sites to help disseminate your messages to a wide audience with no extra effort. Consider also opt-in email marketing for prospective parents, and email communication with current parents.

How do you go about advertising? The best way to factor advertising in to your marketing is to plan it in advance, in order to secure good rates with publications. This also enables implementation, and particularly campaign management, to become more streamlined. Through forward-planning, at least one school has been able to make a 40% saving on projected advertising costs (based on like-for-like coverage).

Forward planning, in the shape of having a clear policy on twice yearly publication and advertising plan reviews, can also help you to manage the number of 'late space' and 'new publication introduction' phone calls that you have to deal with on a day-to-day basis. However, it is also sensible to have a contingency budget, so that if any new advertising opportunity comes along that really fits your situation, you can take advantage of it.

Take the time to have your advertisements designed by an agency that will ensure they are brand-aligned. They should also feature professional photography to maintain the brand message through imagery and words.

Set up a list of target media (and review it regularly). Use your press releases effectively: along with other elements of the marketing mix, they can be used to dispel negative perceptions of the school that you may have learnt about in earlier research.

For instance, if your school undeservedly has a reputation for not having a focus on sport, ensure that all sports successes are followed with a press release to the local paper. Don't write off the smaller community publications that can play an important role in promoting schools and can often have a very loyal and influential following.

Well-written and carefully targeted articles can increase your profile in the local and regional area, or even nationally. The most powerful approach in this respect is to write topic-specific pieces that will be of general interest and establish you as an expert in your field, whether it be a nursery, boarding, or single sex education. Developing a series of articles in, as well as strong relationships with, your target publications will also stand you in good stead as you seek to develop a long-term strategy for raising your school's profile. Profiling specific teachers or the Head can also build brand awareness and show the school's personality to prospective parents.

Community engagement is important too: your school is a part of the community within which it resides, particularly if your core intake is drawn from it. You might consider whether any community events could be held at the school to build interest and awareness, or whether you can sponsor events held in the community. Every contact that anyone in the wider community has with the school should reflect positively on it: such contacts are key ingredients in your ongoing success – so you must engage not only the marketing and admissions team, but also the Head, governors and all staff.

Each member of staff is, in his or her own way, a marketer for the school. Do they all know the key brand messages? Have they seen the new website and advertising schemes? Termly updates for all staff on the marketing activities is a good way to disseminate this information and to encourage stakeholder buy-in.

Signage, livery, exhibitions and uniforms have their parts to play, too. School signage – including entrance signs and way-finding – is important at giving the right first impression. Think of the journey from prospectus to website to first visit: work on your continuity of message and appearance. Think also about staff uniforms (consistent and branded); entrance halls (decked out with inspirational artwork and key messages); drama corridors (with pictures of past school productions); school minibuses (a moving advert whose impact should be maximised through innovative sign writing); banners and other external promotions.

Do the pupils wear a uniform? If so, is it in line with the brand identity? Are your exhibition graphics giving the right impression, and are the messages tailored to the target market, whether it be a local community fair in this country, or an international schools' fair abroad?

Underpinning all of this is the customer journey that makes or breaks the efforts of marketing. Here, as always, it is about attention to detail: how many rings before the telephone is answered; how courteously and helpfully is it answered; continuity of contact during the admissions process; ease of visiting; speed and quality of the prospectus package being sent out. Deliver what you promise – every time. Remember that your target market is exposed to the high standards of corporate marketing and customer relationship management, so your enquirers will enter the relationship with you with the same level of expectation.

You will, of course, want to review all these elements regularly. Re-analysis, review and innovation should be relentlessly on-going. Parents; pupils; the school itself; the business environment; technology and marketing techniques all change over time, so your marketing strategy and implementation should adapt to changing circumstances, enabling you to retain your competitive edge.

Now that you have a route map (even though it will need to be adapted along the way), you can start to implement your strategy and analyse those all-important results. Be realistic when goal setting, but do also set targets and monitor results. This will give you a powerful pool of information on which to base future marketing and to secure appropriate budgets from your governing body. Ensure track-ability as much as you can.

This can be harder to achieve when it comes to more traditional methods, although it is worth asking where all enquiries originate from, and recording and analysing this data long-term. Online, Google Analytics is a powerful tool for measuring not only basic traffic patterns and usage of your site, but also for monitoring response to email marketing campaigns and online marketing. Review the successes and failures of your marketing initiatives, and use these to inform future marketing.

In summary:

- Be knowledgeable. Know your school, your target market and your point of difference.
- Be creative, innovative and memorable. Every touch point with the school is an opportunity to shine, to promote and to get your message heard.
- Be controlled. Relish your role as 'brand guardian' in helping to shape the way the school is perceived.
- Be truthful to the specific characteristics of the school. If yours is not a Facebook school, don't go down this route.
- Be realistic. You can't do everything, so prioritise and call in the professionals where you can, particularly to work on those areas that require specialist knowledge.
- Be accountable. Measure the results and be prepared to change your route if a particularly message or activity is not proving effective.
- Be proactive. Don't sit still. Your competitors won't.

In all of this, consider the customer journey as being of key importance. Whether prospective or current parent or pupil, the journey should be engaging, stimulating, consistently branded and effective. The right branding and key messages will serve not only to attract prospective parents and pupils, but also to retain current parents and pupils and to attract the right staff. Once you have these key principles under your belt, you can go on to manage the brand to full effect and achieve real satisfaction from the results.

Chapter 8

Initial enquiries, open days and personal visits

Individual and group visits are an integral part of the admissions process. In this chapter, two experienced practitioners share their experience across the age range – one with very young children and the other with pupils in senior schools.

Very young children

Deborah Russell

The phone rings, or an email pops up in the inbox. The parent of a baby, toddler or six year-old has heard about your school and would like some more information. This is arguably the most important point in the admissions process. When you answer that phone or respond to that email, it is essential to be welcoming and interested, no matter how frenetic things are in your office.

Your response will probably determine whether an enquiry becomes a visit, which could result in a registration and, hopefully, another pupil in your school. It is worth spending a couple of minutes establishing a relationship. The information that you are given can be very useful: is the family relocating to the area (is this imminent or just a vague plan for the future); what are their child's interests; which school does their child currently attend?

Ensure that there are enquiry forms easily to hand; it is all too easy to forget to ask a crucial question – such as what their contact number is. It is also far too easy to lose a Post-it note bearing scribbled details about a prospective family. Remember to ask how the enquirer knows of your school and how s/he found its phone number. This is very useful information as it will help shape your future marketing. It can reveal the best media for placing adverts and inform your use of websites/search engine optimisation.

Aim to send out the prospectus within 24 hours, with a personalised covering letter inviting the family to arrange a visit or attend your next open day. And if you haven't heard within a couple of days, just give them a call to check it has arrived and maybe to book a tour of the school for them.

The step from contacting a school for information to making a visit can be a very big one for some parents. They can be far more tentative than we expect, especially if we ourselves have had school-aged children and/or are very familiar with the system. Attending an open event can provide prospective parents with an opportunity to get a feel for the school informally, and if prospective parents gain a good impression they will then take things further.

Open days take many forms. If your school has a senior section, you may be part of a whole school event, but it is worth holding a separate one for the parents of younger children. Something essentially informal; possibly a working morning with tours escorted by the oldest pupils; possibly a themed event such as an open afternoon – with a teddy bears' picnic if you are targeting very young children – works very well.

Think carefully about the best time to hold it. If you decide on a working day, your pupils will then be around in the normal course of events. If, however, you are a Monday to Friday school and you choose a Saturday, do you want at least some of the children present? Does your school feel as inspiring without them? Probably not. But don't forget, if you want pupils to be in school on a Saturday, you will need to give their parents plenty of notice.

Advertising your open event will involve rather more than an insert in the local press and a bold banner on your website homepage. Consider the families you are trying to attract. Flyers to playgroups; your local NCT branch; ante-natal clinic; baby-wear store; recreation centre and library (especially if it runs a story-time session) can all pay dividends.

Try to cultivate good relationships with all such contacts throughout the year: word-of-mouth is your best marketing tool.

On the day, clear signage, ample car parking and an obvious reception point are essential. And what about all those buggies? You may need a parking area for them too! A school should always be clean, but a buzzing, thriving community will inevitably result in a little untidiness during each day. Ask someone to do a last minute check. The visitors' lavatory should be monitored regularly during the event too: first impressions matter.

Visiting families may be anxious: they will need to feel welcomed right from the start. Some parents may have disliked their own school; others may never have set foot in a private/maintained school before and may have all sorts of misconceptions. When your visitors arrive, make a note of their contact details so that you can follow up after the day itself with an invitation to arrange a personal visit and perhaps to attend another event such as a fireworks night, concert or Christmas fair. You may choose to have a printed programme, but you should briefly explain the format for the day anyway.

Introduce the family to their tour guide. Older pupils are great ambassadors: they usually charm visitors with their memories of their time in, and enthusiasm for, their school. Make sure they are prepared with a planned route (suited to the age of the prospective pupils) but don't over-rehearse them or they will not come across as natural. If you have strength in a particular area, or a facility of which you are especially proud, ensure that visitors experience it during their tour. Aim to have some activities taking place that visiting children can try.

You may want your Head to make a short address to visitors during the day. Whether s/he does or not, the Head, a few staff members and some current parents should be available over refreshments to chat and to answer questions. Satisfied current parents can be one of your greatest marketing tools, so involve them in the process. Their participation will also underline their valued contribution to the school, both to those parents themselves and to the prospective parents with whom they are engaging.

Finally, when your visitors depart, make sure they receive a proper goodbye and leave with a prospectus, maybe a small memento and a warm invitation to return for a personal visit.

A personal visit is an exciting and sometimes anxious occasion for some prospective parents too, so do everything you can to put them at their ease. Give clear instructions about parking and where to report on arrival. The reception staff should be expecting them; the waiting area should be spotless, warm and well-lit – with a scrapbook of press cuttings about the school; the most recent newsletter or school magazine; an eye catching display of children's work and possibly a toy box to keep the youngest visitor happy for a few minutes.

Tours should not be identical and stereotyped: each should be tailored to the individual family – although there will be common elements. This is where the information gleaned during that initial enquiry conversation comes in useful. Parents looking for a place for their sports-mad seven year-old will not want to linger in the nursery, but they will remember the coaching they witnessed in the cricket nets; their chat with the enthusiastic young sports master; the trophy cabinet.

Those with a toddler will want to spend more time in the early years' department and perhaps will see only the highlights of the upper school – the library, ICT suite and science room – especially if they have their toddler in tow. By the time their two year-old reaches the upper school, much may have changed. Meanwhile the attention span of their two year-old is short!

Who escorts your visitors? Have you accompanied a tour to check that the deputy head/admissions secretary/pre-prep leader is presenting the school in the best possible way? Do they introduce some of the staff (and do they recognise the best ambassadors, such as the most enthusiastic Year 1 teacher, rather than her more earnest colleague?) Can they answer all the most frequently asked questions? Do they keep to schedule?

Every prospective parent wants to meet the Head, so ensure that the family spends some time with him or her, preferably *after* the tour when they can ask questions based on what they have seen. Make sure that you brief the Head on the family beforehand; from the Head's knowledgeable conversation your visitors will appreciate that their visit is seen as being important to the school.

Marketing is part of the remit of every member of the school, from the caretaker to the cook; the nursery nurse to the head of maths; the pupils to the current parents. Make sure they appreciate this. A smile and a cheery hello as they see parents on a tour can be the deciding factor on whether that family feels your school is the right one.

After the visit has taken place, send a follow-up note thanking the parents for coming. Personalise it if possible (we hope the piano exam went well/you enjoy your forthcoming holiday/your relocation goes smoothly) to show that the family is valued by the school. If a registration is not immediately forthcoming, keep in contact – but without the family feeling harassed. Send the termly or annual newsletter, or invite them to a suitable event. Parents with very young families often visit a number of schools with their baby and then return to a couple of them again a year or more later before deciding where to enrol. They are more likely to keep your school in mind if you have kept in touch with them.

Post-registration, the receipt of the completed enrolment form and registration fee is not the end of the story! Parents may register a baby two or more years before that child is due to join your school and they often put their son's or daughter's name down at more than one school too. You need to nurture this new relationship to ensure it is *your* school that the child eventually joins.

Consider holding a yearly afternoon for registered children with, for example, face painting and a bouncy castle, or a weekly parent and toddler group or music session. The families then begin to feel part of the school and their children will be more likely to join you. There is then a good chance that the parents will tell their friends about their positive experience, too.

Senior schools

Muna Ausat

Three key opportunities for any senior school marketer are open days, personal visits and admissions procedures. Getting them right is hardly rocket science, but you need careful planning and attention to detail to make a success of it. Remember that you will be judged every step of the way.

One of the first rules of marketing is knowing who your audience is. This is particularly important when recruiting into senior schools as the older the pupil, the more say s/he is likely to have in the final decision. I am increasingly organising tours for families whose parents know very little about us. Their daughter on the other hand has already 'chosen' my college, because she has attended a netball tournament or one of our thinking skills activity days. So my job is already half done.

When staging the perfect open day, all the obvious rules apply. Make sure your school looks as good as it can: displays should be vibrant and tidy, of course, with no loose borders or curled edges. Make sure you have plenty of pupils' work on display (as well as photographs and exam results, *etc*). Pupils and staff should look their best, and be friendly and welcoming. Remember everybody is a marketer! Have lots of mini-activities for your younger visitors.

But what is it that is really going to set you apart from the competition, when everyone nowadays has a state-of-the-art 'this' and the latest 'that'? Ultimately it is going to be the actual experience of the event that will sway them, from the moment they make that first phone call, through the assessment process until they accept an offer of a place and pay that hefty deposit.

Decisions, decisions, decisions! Who will conduct the tour of the prospective families: will it be you or your pupils? Will there be an opportunity to meet the Head? There is no right or wrong answer to this: different schools will have different approaches, but as a general rule parents enjoy being shown round by a pupil, especially on an open day, and they tend to understand that this may not be possible when they come for a personal visit during the school day. (It is of course easier to arrange pupil tours in larger schools, where sixth-formers have free periods.)

Some schools offer Head's tours, involving half-an-hour or so with the Head and a group of other parents, followed by a pupil-led tour. The advantage of this is that parents feel important and (dare I say it!) it shows that the Head acknowledges his/her marketing role. A major disadvantage is that parents would have to fit in with the tour dates and times, rather than being able to book a visit when it suits them. At my school parents really appreciate our flexible approach to personal visits – but it cannot be an option for the Heads of medium-sized and large schools which are recruiting large numbers of pupils each year.

Formal talks: who will give them, and how long is too long? At an open day the Head's talk is highly important. Think carefully about the timings and how many times s/he should speak at one event: you will need to consider how long a tour lasts, and whether you can fit one in both before and after the Head speaks.

As a mother of three boys, 17, 15 and nine, I have been to many open days (and I shall still have to go to more). Although I am interested in what the Head has to say, the people from whom I really want to hear are the pupils. This is where it is really important to consider your audience. Too often Heads take their open day speech to be an opportunity to talk at length about *themselves, their* vision and *their* school.

This is where pupil speeches can be deployed to great advantage. The head boy/girl should make parents want their own child to be just like them – confident, articulate, clever and a great role model. But consider getting Year 7 or Year 8 pupils to talk too. They will be able to engage your younger audience and understand their concerns: how will I settle in; will I make friends; how will I find my way around such a big school?

Refreshments: open days can be very tiring, so it's only right to offer your visitors something tasty from the dining room. It's also a great way to showcase the quality of your catering provision. The refreshment area is a good place to show your DVD or a PowerPoint presentation filled with images of happy pupils doing lots of wonderful things. Visitors will have a moment to take these in.

Follow up: there are different ways of dealing with this. You can either ask your visitors to book in advance for an event, or get them to fill in a form when they arrive. The trick is to capture as much information as possible. Armed with this information, you can then send out feedback forms about your open day. Having done this, I always then discuss the findings at the open day *post mortem*: another essential meeting that you should hold after every event. Once you have these details you can stay in regular contact and send out newsletters and invitations to special events. You are building that all important relationship.

However, when it comes to personal visits, other tactics ap. and carry out most of the tours at my school: it's one of my favourite jobs. This is my chance to show my school off and help set it apart from the competition.

When parents book a visit, try to get as much information about them and their child as possible, without being intrusive. Make sure the receptionist knows who is coming and greets all visitors by name. If the prospective pupil is present, ask what its favourite subjects are so that you can focus on those areas of the school first. Parents love this! Be as honest as possible when dealing with difficult or awkward questions. If you don't know the answer, try to find someone to ask along the way or at the end of the tour. If no one can help, arrange to contact the parent later with an answer – and it is essential to follow this up quickly.

How flexible you are, and how easy it is for a parent to book a personal visit, are also very important. Remember, you will be compared to the competition and judged constantly. Nowadays, schools have to take a much more customer-focused approach than in the past. Remember you are asking parents to part with large sums of money in return for a first-class education for their child and they should expect high standards of customer service from you.

When considering admissions procedures, it is again important to consider your audience. Are these parents first time buyers? Are you dealing with a father and a mother who may have different priorities? An increasing number of first time buyers are often unsure of themselves, coming with many, many questions and not always familiar with a lot of the terminology that people use in the independent sector. The trick is to be clear, concise and open.

Teamwork: the registrar and the marketing director must work together. Registrars must be very efficient and professional, seeming never to mind how many times they are asked the same question and how often they have to reassure parents. It's a tough job dealing often with distraught parents who are desperate for a place, or having to inform parents that their son or daughter has not passed the entrance test.

IAL ENQUIRIES, OPEN DAYS AND PERSONAL VISITS

...y of information: whether you are operating as a school on your own or a consortium, make sure that your test/exam and interview dates ow.ed and published well in advance – along with dates when offer letters will be posted and when acceptances will be required. In this way parents know well in advance what to expect and the procedure is transparent.

On the exam day itself you have yet another marketing opportunity. Don't treat it as just another routine part of the process. Some candidates will have been up long before dawn; some parents, fearful of traffic jams (even on a Saturday), will have allowed an hour for what is normally a 20-minute journey. Make sure that you have prefects or older pupils on hand to meet and reassure candidates and parents as they arrive, and to talk to them in that tense waiting period before the more laid-back parents and candidates eventually turn up.

Most candidates will have pre-exam nerves, and many may want to go to the (clearly signposted) facilities. Once they have gone off to their first exam, recognise that parents will still be anxious and offer them coffee and a place to relax: this is a good time for you or the Head to explain to them that even the most nervous candidate is usually fine, once the first exam begins. Once again make sure your displays are highly visible and well-cared-for, and that you and the registrar are on hand to answer any last-minute questions.

Later, when you make your offers, remember that parents have a choice. Congratulate them on their child's success and remind them how well s/he has done to get into your school.

And finally, be prepared to offer 'decision tours': the opportunity for parents to have just one more look around the school before accepting an offer. They feel empowered, because now they hold an offer and it's up to us to convince them to take it up.

Consider sending newsletters to parents and children in the months between a place being accepted and their actual arrival in the school. When admission is imminent, it's time to send the information pack and arrange an induction visit for the child – either on an individual basis or as a group exercise just before the start of the new term.

Consider also holding a 'welcome meeting' for all the new parents; an informal social event where they can meet the staff and other new parents and ask any questions they may have. And on the child's first day, ensure each family is met on arrival and guided to the classroom, even though they will have already visited it. The more at ease they feel, the better their impression of the school.

Finally, after the first couple of weeks, send a friendly letter to the new families asking for feedback on their experience of the whole admissions process. They won't all reply, but those who do may highlight some small thing that the school could have done to make their experience easier. They will appreciate being asked their opinion and, if you adjust your procedure accordingly, subsequent families – and the school – will benefit.

Remember that there is no right or wrong way, but we all learn from experience – and from feedback.

Chapter 9

Recruitment and retention of sixth-formers

With a rising awareness amongst parents and pupils of all the choices available between schools and across both the independent and maintained sectors, retention has become a much more significant issue than it once was – especially at sixth form level.
A day school Head and the marketing and admissions director at a school recruiting boarders give two perspectives on the challenges that this situation presents.

Day schools

Edward Elliott

I am a child of Thatcher's Britain, and I grew up with the idea that privatisation and competition are necessary pre-requisites to success. There is nothing quite like a Darwinian struggle for survival to keep an institution on its toes, and to ensure continuous improvement. The theory is fine: the reality a little less comfortable.

For the last 13 years I have worked at the Perse School in Cambridge, first as head of sixth form, then as deputy head and more recently as Head. The Perse operates in a very competitive, but thankfully growing, day school market, but it faces competition from four excellent independent schools and an outstanding (and free) sixth form college. Cambridge sixth-formers operate in a buyer's market in which they have a wonderful cornucopia of educational choice. They complete a grand tour of sixth form open evenings every autumn before deciding on their first choice institution.

Against this competitive background, the Perse has been very successful in growing sixth form numbers, which have more than doubled over the last decade to 300 plus. What follows is some advice that may have generic value in helping schools recruit and retain sixth-formers.

The first big question is: do you recruit or do you retain? Some big companies focus too much on sales targets and forget that dull purchasing efficiencies can have a much bigger effect on the bottom line. In a similar way schools can be seduced by recruitment drives and can forget the importance of retention. Retention is often the best option – you know who you are getting: their strengths and weaknesses, and what they have been taught.

The latter is of increasing importance in the diverse world of Year 11 qualifications, and it can be a major challenge to bring GCSE and IGCSE new entrants up to the same starting point for an AS course that has to be crammed into two-and-a-bit school terms. Of course, there will be pupils who do not fit with an institution, and in these cases it is better to stand aside and let them leave. Fees may be lost, but the cost will not be as high as having disaffected sixth-formers creating problems for two years to come.

Recruiting, meanwhile, can be an excellent way of bringing new academic and extracurricular blood into the sixth form. A cohort of hard working and capable new sixth form entrants can have a remarkable impact on year group culture, and thus on exam results and league table positions; a six foot seven England schoolboy No 8 can revive the fortunes of the 1st XV. That said, remember that students leave schools for good and bad reasons and that, if you are not discerning, you can end up recruiting problem cases off-loaded with relief by other schools.

In some cases this may be the right thing to do; the pupils concerned may fit in better to your institution and may finally realise all their potentials, but it is not *always* so. Do not ignore your pastoral and academic instincts purely in order to achieve your recruitment targets – assuming of course that you have the luxury of not having to recruit *all* enquirers simply in order to survive.

There are two elements to recruitment and retention which are often blurred but which do require different skills. These are marketing and

105

sales. Marketing the sixth form is a job for a professional marketer: a qualified professional who understands market research, demographics, advertising campaigns, focus groups, market positioning and competitor analysis. You can't market a school effectively until you understand its market, and recognise that those markets are dynamic. Markets do not stand still, and you need to keep ahead of changing market trends and the competition. It is better to be proactive than reactive to issues such as curriculum reform and university admission.

Professional marketers have the training to calculate market size: to predict how population and economic changes will affect market potential; to research the market and to find out how your school is perceived; to be mystery shoppers at competitor institutions; to carry out market surveys of current parents and students to find out their views. Once the market has been mapped, a target market can be identified and then strategies identified to reach the chosen audience.

Target markets need to be large enough to sustain the school, and relatively free from competition; competition might be a good thing, but over-competition isn't – and too many schools in too small a niche market will result in failure. Marketing strategies will involve the articulation of clear messages: core values that will define your niche in the market, and communication measures to reach your target audience.

At sixth form level, a key market research question is: who decides post-16 choice (pupil, parents, or combination, but in what ratio?) and when do they decide? My own experience is that sixth form decisions are often made in Year 10. Research also needs to identify the key controls of decision-making, which could be: quality of teaching; peer group pressure and friendship groups; parents; curriculum; facilities; ethos; academic results; university offers; fashion (schools do indeed go in and out of fashion); extracurricular activities; fees; single sex or coeducation, institutional size. The quality and size of your sixth form centre, and the facilities enjoyed by senior pupils there, also help. The list is not exhaustive, and for many pupils it will be a combination of the above that influences their post-16 decision-making.

Once the market strategy has been refined by a professional marketer, sales work can begin. Sixth form selling is the work of teachers and students because they have the skills needed to communicate with the customers. In an independent day school with a small, well-defined catchment area (both by geography and socio-economic status), selling is largely a word of mouth business.

Positive words in the Waitrose coffee shop; a buzz in local sports clubs and good feedback on Facebook will work wonders. The last is a particularly powerful tool for sixth form recruitment and retention, but one that cannot be easily controlled. The Twitter or Facebook friendship groups can promote or damn a school in the pupil consciousness.

The best advice is to run a good school: if students are happy and successful they will share this on the internet. However, if there are problems, your dirty washing will be all round the town. In a salutary way, the Facebook revolution makes the quality of day-to-day pupil educational experience more important than a sales and marketing campaign: it ensures that substance triumphs over style.

Aside from word-of-mouth, selling the school is best done through events such as open evenings and one-to-one tours and meetings. The best sixth form open evenings are busy and vibrant. As with restaurants, a full sixth form event creates the impression that this is the place to be; that the apparent popularity is well earned, and that all these visitors can't be wrong.

It is, however, a balancing act. If you have too many visitors, the open evening can become over-powering, and the school will feel like just another large impersonal sixth form college. Some staff will also need encouragement to sell their subject – and thereby the school, too. They may feel uncomfortable in doing so for fear that this will alienate other departments, but such sensitivities need to be put to one side: open evenings celebrate all that a school does well and everyone should put their best foot forward.

Even more important than staff in the sixth form selling process are current sixth-formers. Their evident enthusiasm for the sixth form can be infectious, and their unrefined positivity very effective – precisely because it comes from the heart. One-to-one tours with existing sixth-formers (carefully chosen) can seal the deal. Prospective pupils and parents really value the current student voice and it needs to be hard, loud and clear – on open days, and through the prospectus and via web videos.

Recruitment events are a reflection of the school, and they need to be well organised, well publicised, and well catered for. Never underestimate the importance of food and drink in the decision-making process: fruit smoothies, chocolate brownies, and marshmallows roasting on an open fire (risk assessed, of course) leave very favourable impressions.

Sixth form prospectuses need to be attractive and professional, and they should occupy a halfway house between university and school publications. Parents want to know that the school has systems and structures to ensure high level academic attainment, while pupils want to see evidence of greater freedoms, more choice, and new opportunities. A sixth form prospectus that looks like a university publication, with lots of appealing photographs but also some serious text to reassure parents about support structures and work ethic, is a winning combination.

Other selling tactics can be used. Introducing new subjects may bring in new students, but beware of increasing staff costs to the point at which you create a loss leader. Remember too that new subjects come and go, and some may never establish themselves. Scholarships can be effective recruitment tools, both in kudos and in monetary value. However, in a post public benefit world their role has diminished and in most day school scenarios the value of the scholarship is unlikely to be a 'deal breaker'. You must also remember that in awarding a scholarship to one student, you risk alienating another who feels that justice has not been done. Alienated pupils often go elsewhere, and they can take their friends with them.

Finally, do not underestimate the value of some age-old concepts. A sixth form taught by staff who manifestly enjoy the daily banter and engagement with young people, whilst setting them firm boundaries. A well-publicised, Rolls-Royce system for dispensing A level results and university advice. A leavers' day or prize-giving event that channels their excitement and enthusiasm into mutual appreciation and nostalgia by leavers and non-leavers alike, rather than a souring 'muck-up day' (remember too that 11-16 year-olds observe this occasion and draw their own conclusions from it, for better or worse...).

Above all, the 11-18 school with the sixth form working to help young pupils settle in and develop, through the prefect system, is evergreen and ever popular. Even cynical sixth-formers, keen to acquire new facilities, freedoms and privileges, can't resist a little vertical integration and the opportunity to act as big brother or big sister. It is good for the school, good for the pupils, and a very effective niche marketing tool against the 16-18 colleges.

Boarding schools

Erica Town

In some ways, recruiting boarders is no different from attracting day pupils. In order to attract successfully new sixth form pupils (as well as to retain existing fifth-formers), there is a need for clear segmentation of marketing and for tailoring promotional campaigns to this specific group – something that is often overlooked. It is important to recognise that this target group is different from your general recruitment (be it at 11 or 13). For this age-group, there will also be more complex reasons driving a change of school than at an earlier age, so fully understanding these reasons is vitally important.

First, look at your leavers and analyse the reasons that pupils and parents give as to why they are leaving or looking for a new school. Then think what this information is telling you about your 'product', and the way in which you present and 'sell' your sixth form internally.

Secondly, bear in mind that for those wanting to join you, it is often the pupil who is driving the change, with either parental backing or resistance. In the end, almost certainly it will be the pupil who has the final say about where next. So the task of drawing up the marketing messages that appeal to both parents and 16 year-olds is a tricky one.

For both groups it is therefore important, in communication terms, to combine messages (for teenagers) about the benefits that the school offers to senior boarders with (for parents) the attractive potential exam results and university outcomes.

Fortunately, finding out what appeals to 17-18 year-old boarders is not difficult, because you have a captive market on your doorstep: your current pupils. Talk to them either informally, by having lunch with them or visiting them in their houses, or more formally via a set of focus groups. One particular group to focus on is those boarders who came in at sixth form level from other schools, as they will tell you better than anyone about their selection criteria and why they came. Some of this information will be generic, but certainly you will also find a myriad of 'little things' that made the difference, and you can build these into your communications and promotion plans, both for existing and for new pupils.

Then, analyse the competition – looking at the other schools or colleges your leavers go to, or which schools your new pupils are coming from. This will give you clues as to the driving factors. The ubiquitous SWOT analysis can be an invaluable tool in helping define and refine your offering.

How do you recruit and retain sixth-formers in a boarding school? Developing the idea of an all-round sixth form experience is one part of the process. Day parents, who would not have entertained the idea of letting their child board at 13, may consider it at 16. Marketing is easier and more cost effective if you can convert your potential leavers and day pupils into boarders, but you need to target them specifically about the benefits of boarding at this stage.

Style and tone of voice are critical for the 16+ age group, and it is a difficult balancing act to get right. However, again you have a captive market in your current sixth form boarders that you can consult over website pieces or advertising. This age group is very marketing/brand savvy, but beware trying to be 'hip' or 'cool' or 'on trend': you will almost always get it wrong!

Would-be sixth-formers will respond well to electronic communication, so think hard about appropriate opportunities via emails: tone and content should be different to those that you may send to parents. However letter post is such a rarity these days that an appropriately designed personal invitation to an open day/evening can score equally well for its novelty and personal approach.

A special section on the website is vital; it allows you to expand on what is unique about boarding in the sixth form. Again, some pieces written by existing pupils will often get the style and tone right, and will talk about the aspects of your school that matter to 17 year-olds, much more effectively than those written by adults. As well as the obvious A level options, results, destinations *etc*, what extras or special aspects do you offer that your competition does not?

What are your unusual subjects and combinations; special extension courses; sports offered/facilities? What kind of boarding provision do you have (sixth form house; shared/single rooms)? What freedoms are there for sixth-formers; how good is the university application and careers advice programme; what are the uniform and extracurricular options and requirements? Do you have wifi easily available to sixth-formers? What are your policies on mobile phones and access to Facebook? How extensive is the weekend programme, and is there any scope for going to social events and parties? All these and more are aspects that matter to this age group.

Advertising should be noticeably different for this target group from that which comprises your general recruitment advertising. Make sure the age group of pupils shown in photographs is right and think about the key messages you want to convey: you should know this from your internal research. Perhaps they centre around academic results and university choices, or maybe around wider issues of independence and freedom, or sport/work balance?

What are the specific opportunities offered through the boarding experience *over and above* those that good day schools can provide? These may include the making of deep and lasting friendships, and the opportunity to spend time developing skills and interests to a high level (time which might otherwise be expended on stressful daily commuting, both by students themselves and by parents bringing them to, or picking them up from, school).

Can you make a point of the fact that, when you take the costs of travel and food/heat and light into account, the costs of boarding compared with day education start to look less dramatic than they seem at first sight? Do you have spaces to offer flexi-boarding as well as the traditional variety?

Specific information on your website tailored to your overseas pupil body is another must. If you have large numbers of one nationality, and want more of them, a translation is probably well worth the investment – although it does not need to cost you a huge amount as, once again, your own pupils should be able to assist.

Do not underestimate the time it takes them to do a high quality translation and think about timescales that will not conflict with their school work. Offer some kind of reward, even if it is not a pecuniary one – for instance, book tokens or a weekend or evening outing. It is also a good idea to get a few of your overseas parents to contribute messages about their enthusiasm for your school too.

What scholarship/bursary schemes do you have for the sixth form? Do you spell out the selection criteria; the timetable for application; the number of awards available? Or is it all buried somewhere deep in the website? Is it a matter of chance about when you apply?

There is no fixed answer as to whether to hold a separate open day-type event for new sixth form boarders: it depends in part on the distance from which you recruit your market, and on the number of places available. In promoting your boarding, taster days with an overnight stay provide the opportunity for potential pupils to get to know their peer group and 'to hear it like it is'. This will do more to sell the school than a marketing-led event, but if you are looking for large numbers, this more personal approach may not always be practical.

Meanwhile, you will be keen to retain most, if not all, of your current pupils. However good your sixth form package may be, it is inevitable that after many years in (say) a three to 18 school, some pupils will 'just want a change'. For some, perhaps you do not offer the subject choices they are looking for, while a few may not make the sixth form entry requirements.

Analysis of historic data will show you the 'normal' number of leavers for each year. If you have more than 10% leaving in Year 11, there is either a problem lower down the school or your sixth form experience is not right. For the 'just want a change' group, there is a limit to what you can do to retain them, but whether it is a trickle or a flood there are some key things you should do on an annual basis.

Much of what follows could be used as a checklist for retaining day pupils as much as boarders, but in the current economic and social climate, it is the boarding market that we can least afford to take for granted.

- First and foremost, what have you actually done in marketing terms to retain current boarders beyond a (perhaps) pretty dull evening about A level choices?
- Was there a vibrant presentation about what else comes with the sixth form package?
- Have you set up a sixth form presentation event for current pupils and parents, with existing sixth-formers involved in the process?
- Have you conducted an exit interview or a leavers' survey with both pupils and parents, to get consistent and regular feedback? Both groups are likely to be forthright as they are leaving!
- Have you talked to your current sixth-formers, and those new to the school, to see whether the 'product' is living up to expectations?
- Have you talked to house parents about the more informal feedback they may have received and what issues and concerns they have?

Of course, as a marketer, you cannot necessarily change the sixth form 'product', but your research work can inform the senior management team (SMT) when it is considering future changes that will help retain more current pupils and, as a consequence, attract new ones too. In addition to the academic offering what other differences are there?

- What real benefits are there to being a sixth-former? What responsibilities or new 'freedoms' do they get, over and above the rest of the school? Too often the head boy/girl, prefect or monitor roles are little more than 'gofers' and do not live up to the hype.
- How involved are the boarding pupils in the way the boarding 'product' evolves?
- Are there different uniform requirements to those lower down the school: for example, none at all, or suits rather than blazers?
- Are there special outings/events? City-based schools clearly have an advantage over those out in the country for this target group – so, if

you are one of the latter, are you putting on enough opportunities of this type to ensure that boarding sixth-formers do not feel they are missing out?

• What do you offer in co-curricular terms that really appeals to this age group?

• What do you do to keep them in touch with normal every day teenage life?

There is a mix of opinion as to whether through-age boarding houses or sixth-form-only ones are the best option. Certainly if your school goes for the former, you need to work harder to create distinctions that reflect the age of the pupils and give an increasing sense of freedom and responsibility for older pupils. What 'preparation for university' sessions do you have? Cooking, washing, budgeting can all be part of the sixth form experience and positive 'training' for all: this provision will appeal to parents, too.

All in all, whether it's improving retention of your current boarders or external recruitment, the key is a clearly differentiated 'sixth form experience product': well-articulated, well-communicated and, moreover, actually delivered in reality.

To retain pupils, a school needs its sixth-formers to enjoy a different relationship with the school than the one had between the ages of 11 and 16, and this needs to be 'sold' as persuasively to current pupils and parents as to new prospects. School for these two years should be an 'enrichment' process for all involved: staff; pupils; parents. It should come with noticeable benefits and educational extras and should be a genuine step change.

To retain existing, and to attract new, boarding pupils, you need to analyse carefully what you really are offering in the sixth form, and to make sure that you communicate it effectively to both target groups. So often schools are delivering a good 'product' but are failing to communicate enough differentiated aspects that are both relevant and appealing, or described in enough detail to both those in, and those outside, the school.

Chapter 10

The marketing of boarding

Recruiting boarders presents special challenges. This chapter explores the question in two different respects: first, attracting pupils who already live in the UK, and then those from abroad.

UK customers

Henrietta Lightwood

There are now 511,886 girls and boys who are at ISC member schools. Of these, 67,856 (13.3%) are boarders. Out of 1260 ISC schools, 39% offer boarding. However only 10% of these are predominantly boarding. Recent developments in the boarding market include the opening of 35 state boarding schools and the increase in international students who, in 2010, now make up over 30% of boarders (23,307) in UK schools. If, however, you look at it from the opposite perspective, the other 70% are pupils already in the UK – so the good news is that there is definitely a market for UK boarding. However, amongst all this competition how do you make your boarding school stand out from the crowd?

Perhaps the first question to ask is: why do UK parents want to send their children to board? Having nurtured their offspring at home for many years, why do some parents decide to send their children away to school, to be looked after by 'other people' and to live communally with other pupils where they share bedrooms, bathroom facilities and common rooms? Is this not an outdated concept, more akin to the Victorian era where children were seen and not heard?

By contrast of course, boarding these days is very much suited to 21st century family needs and schools have adapted extensively, becoming very modern in outlook. UK parents are working longer hours, often in exceedingly demanding jobs, and they are uneasy about their teenagers roaming the streets after they finish at their day school.

Others may be posted overseas where the standards of local education are often not up to what they have previously taken for granted in Britain. For some families boarding is a tradition: part of growing up; being independent; a rite of passage. For others, it is a place where their children can be safe, enjoy their childhood and avoid being forced to grow up too quickly. As a marketer, it is important to understand the motivation of your parents.

Boarding schools have had to adapt. In the better schools, facilities are top notch: fabulous study bedrooms; modern bathrooms; internet access; Skype; food to suit a variety of different pallets; multimedia common rooms and, of course, your own tennis court and swimming pool to use at the weekend. Boarding staff have gone on courses in advocacy and counselling. They are both parents and friends to pupils, not only dealing with friendship problems, safeguarding children and parental communication, but also organising weekend risk assessments, devising a myriad of trips and activities and deal with a lack of sleep. Those of us who work in the sector know how good boarding can be, and how much things have changed over time, but the challenge is conveying these messages to our potential customers.

Parental choice and customer service is king. "Shall we full or weekly board?" "Can my daughter/son flexi- or occasional board?" The questions we, as marketers, should be asking are: what do we as schools offer; how are we different to other schools; have we got our offer right, and is it value for money?

Anyone involved in the marketing of a boarding school has to start with sound market research. For this you can either use an external consultancy or do some desktop research yourself. Find out what your current parents and pupils value about their boarding experience. What do they like, and dislike, about it? What prompted them to start boarding and why did they chose your particular school? Are there any gaps between expectation and reality for those new to boarding? Are they going to stay in boarding school for the duration of their school years?

Survey your staff to find out what they feel about the boarding experience they provide and visit other schools. How does what you offer compare? Are there any lessons that could be learned?

Many UK boarders will come from prep schools where there is a long tradition of boarding. Most prep school pupils will already have flexi- or occasionally boarded: these pupils and their parents will be comfortable with schools that have a boarding ethos. Many of these parents will be looking for a full boarding school with lots to do and many weekend activities. Find out which these schools are, and which ones have sent pupils to you in the past.

Cultivate relationships with them and make sure they understand what your school offers. Support prep schools by giving feedback on their ex-pupils who may have achieved great things when they went on to your school. If a child gains a scholarship, let the prep school know so that it can celebrate the success with the child and can use this as a marketing opportunity itself. Advertise in their school magazines, concert programmes or open day leaflets. Support their events; speak at their speech days and participate in their senior school exhibitions. Try inviting them to prep school events at your school such as science days, sports matches or art workshops, so that they can see for themselves the activities that would be beneficial for their pupils.

Forces' parents regularly posted overseas receive the continuity of education allowance (CEAS), which goes a substantial way towards paying boarding fees. Some schools offer Forces discounts in addition, to encourage children from such families to attend their school. There are many advertising opportunities both off and online to target the military: agencies that will represent schools on garrison tours; organisations that direct mail to HIVEs (an information/relocation service for armed forces' personnel and their families). The Forces themselves organise school fairs. Being near a military base generally helps and schools that are in this category can benefit from good junior boarding numbers. However the location of grandparents or good friends is often a key consideration.

Never underestimate dinner party conversation. Forces parents are great communicators and if one family finds a good school, the likelihood is that they will recommend it to a friend. Some schools offer their pupils the chance to be part of a cadet scheme, which they market to Forces parents. Others offer the Duke of Edinburgh's Award or particular sports.

As with any prospective pupil, there are some Forces families that will only opt for a co-ed school, whereas others may be more comfortable with single-sex arrangements. Giving their children a stable and secure place to live, particularly if the family has moved on a regular basis, is a paramount concern. Cementing friendships; the prospect of good GCSEs, stability and continuity of care often make boarding the only sensible option.

Meanwhile, don't disregard your day parents, thinking that they will never switch. They are already your customers and it may be easier to 'sell up' rather than 'recruit new'. Even those dyed in the wool 'I could never let my child be looked after by another adult apart from me' types often change their tune when the teenage years commence!

For those with time-consuming sporting or musical commitments, staying over on a Wednesday night could be a preferred option to lots of travelling. Many parents welcome the option of a weekend away without their children and are pleased that they can be in a safe environment with lots of weekend activities, surrounded by their friends. Others may have occasional work commitments that take them away for weeks at a time and don't have grandparents or a support network to call on.

Whatever the reason, encourage your current and prospective pupils to come in for a trial session and, when they do, make it fun! Most young people like spending time with their friends; going for sleepovers; enjoying activities in a group environment or going on trips together. This is what boarding is all about. Put on such good weekend trips that your day pupils are envious of the boarders and want to come to join in. Cover the events with photographs, website and newsletter stories; perhaps there may even be a local press story. Talk about it and celebrate it: enthusiasm is infectious.

Day parents may also consider flexi-boarding as an option when their children go into the sixth form. Some feel this is an ideal preparation for university; for their children to gain independence and a tolerance of others before they live completely on their own. Perhaps it can be an opportunity for them to practise washing their own clothes or trying out their cooking skills; to start to control their own time and to work to deadlines. Produce booklets or leaflets targeted at your Year 11 day parents, explaining the options and selling the benefits – and ensure that socially there is plenty to do, so that you are creating a healthy balance between safety and freedom.

As a window to the world, your website is of key importance. Consider a website section on boarding where you talk about the boarding experience; the benefits of boarding; your facilities and the activities on offer. Showcase your staff; write pupil case studies and fill your site with regularly updated photographs and newsworthy stories. Link it to sites such as those of the Boarding Schools' Association (BSA), Hobsons and guardianship agencies. Consider a parents' intranet to aid internal communication.

Some schools send weekly email newsletters, showcasing what has been happening in boarding: most will invite prospective pupils to come in for taster nights. There should be a section in your prospectus highlighting your boarding provision – and how about writing age-specific boarding handbooks with sections written by your current boarders? Colourful boarding leaflets and exhibition stands are vital to give out at exhibitions. And, with parental permission of course, consider the use of video material on boarding trips, which you can show at open days, and a boarding school DVD.

Above all, have fun when you're marketing – and talk to other people in school about what you're doing. Your job is really important and a vital one in terms of the school's viability. What you do really *does* make a difference.

* * * *

The international market

Sue Freestone

(with grateful thanks to Felicity Blake and Sarah Bellotti)

The fact that independent schools in the UK are welcoming record numbers of students from overseas is hardly surprising. According to the Organisation for Economic Co-operation and Development (OECD), fee-charging schools in the UK achieve the best results of any type of school in the world. The reasons why British boarding schools achieve these results are many and varied, and it would take a far deeper analysis than is possible in this short chapter to come up with them all.

Nonetheless, from the perspective of those who view us from afar, I suspect that the analysis is fairly simple. When compared to our international competitors, we have very favourable teacher-pupil ratios; our staff are highly qualified professionals; we invest heavily in facilities for sport and the creative and performing arts and we inculcate values that parents hope we will instil in their children. There is no doubt that the history and tradition of the British boarding school are attractive to overseas students and their families.

Fundamentally, international marketing is no different from any other sort, in that the aim is to attract clients; to persuade them to commit and then to ensure that they are so happy with their 'purchase' that they come back for more and recommend the experience to others. This is equally true whether marketing places in mainstream education, an international study centre or summer schools.

That said, the most important principle of any marketing – understanding your client – is central to the overseas market. This begins with thorough research into the culture of any nation to be visited. Inadvertently treading on cultural toes can be costly, and sympathetic engagement with the values and aspirations of others, together with a sensitive and appropriate response to different cultures, is crucially important. Understanding the priorities of different nationalities will inform the delivery of the message, the presentation of the product within each context and the emphasis appropriate to the target market.

The best source of information is clearly a native of the country to be visited – preferably a business professional who speaks good English! Current parents provide a good source of advice – although it can sometimes be a little awkward when approaching them for the first time. However, my experience is that they are only too happy to help, and even to set up meetings with prospective parents when you visit.

In the absence of any current parents, past pupils can be even more effective – and if that fails, agents are always available to provide information, although some can be a tad wary that you might be intending to bypass their system. On the other hand, agents can guide you and alert you to the habits peculiar to individual nationalities. For example, the lateness of some countries to confirm acceptance of offers can be related to climate: one agent from Latvia assured us that parents are reluctant to commit themselves until the snow clears!

Education fairs provide an opportunity to meet agents or parents in a structured and safe environment. Some organisers can be restrictive in what they want you to say, and how they want you to present your information. If they leave you feeling that you have told only half the story, and the least important half at that, do not be afraid of stepping outside the parameters they set. Attendance at education fairs which involve meeting only agents need to be viewed as part of a long-term strategy. Short-term returns are rare.

Our product is perceived to be high quality – even to be the best in the world. It follows, therefore, that there is an expectation that every element of our presentation must be stylish and professional. Shortcuts are not acceptable in the international market. Brochures must be printed on top-quality paper; CDs and DVDs must run according to the specifications of the country. Again, thorough research is essential. If it is your practice to give away 'freebies', they need to be of good quality; anything tacky will drive your potential customers away. Presentations must be slick and well rehearsed and if you rely on technology it is essential to have a contingency plan that carries equal impact.

We are accustomed to selling our product on the basis of subtle, unspoken values and ethos. When presenting overseas we find ourselves subject to a different kind of scrutiny. We have to provide evidence of the quality of our offering and to be prepared to defend a position seldom questioned within the comfort of our own studies. Many parents and agents will appear armed with last summer's league tables and will want to know why your school is not in the top 20. You may know the answers, but you need to be able to defend your position with a melody that attunes itself with the harmony of the questioner.

As in all marketing that relates to the care and education of children, the establishment of trust and an emotional bond is fundamental; even more so overseas, and especially when dealing directly with parents. Empathy with the parent, and an acknowledgement of the enormity of the responsibility they are placing upon you as an individual, combine to bring about a commitment to the school you represent.

In addition to a first class education, it is crucial to convey the message that your school will offer safety, security and effective pastoral care. Parents value 'testimonials' from same-nationality young people as their own, who have benefited from, and succeeded in (not quite the same thing), the UK system. It can be powerful to have an alumnus by your side conveying the truth of your message – first hand and in the language of the receiver.

Realistically, agents offer the main channel for recruiting international students. Therein lies the major difference with regard to overseas marketing – and the greatest challenge, in that you are working with a third party on whom you have to rely to convey your key message effectively. Establishing sound professional working relationships with reliable agents who understand your product takes time and perseverance.

It is important to listen to agents carefully and to focus on those who display a genuine interest in education and the wellbeing of the student. Ideally, they should visit the school and meet the key players in providing education and care. It is equally important to maintain links with those agents you favour; to nurture relationships and to give regular feedback on the students they send. Like all professionals, they appreciate a prompt response and an efficient service.

In 2009 English UK (a language teaching association with all members accredited by the British Council – including private language schools, educational trusts and charities and language centres in further education colleges and universities) completed a survey to find out what agents want. Their main findings were:

- Face-to-face communication with schools/marketing managers.
- 89% of agents use students' feedback in promotion of an agency arrangement – it might be a good idea to provide them with school's students' feedback.
- 76% of agents want 'Certificate of Representation'; agents prefer visual material to lots of text about the school.
- Agents like to be kept up-to-date with students' progress and specifically require a reassuring email in the first week of the student's arrival.
- 96% of agents' information about the UK education system and the UK in general is from the school. How much information do we provide? In what language?
- Agents like attending fairs and workshops to compare what is on offer in an efficient way.

Finally...

An agent feedback questionnaire is an excellent way of finding out how to improve the relationship with agents and also how to repair any short-term damage through, for example, slow payment of commission.

So-called 'Fam trips' (a free or low-cost trip for travel consultants, provided by a travel operator or airline, or school, as a means of promoting their service) and 'inward missions' (funded by those visiting) are excellent ways for agents to meet many similar schools in a particular region – as well as a unique opportunity for the host school to show off all its strengths.

The UK Border Agency (UKBA) requires schools to have documentation on agency agreements and terms and conditions and the school also needs to provide evidence of having checked each agent's credentials (through references, *etc*). Changes to the requirements of the UKBA have been much in the news in recent months. As ever, the ingenuity of those involved has overcome the difficulties for the present but the need to send an unconditional offer has certainly challenged our own entry protocol.

Meanwhile never underestimate the importance of the website. As with our own indigenous market, families frequently seek out schools at the behest of the potential students themselves. They will undoubtedly have done their research via the internet, and our websites must present in a way that is attractive to young people.

As young consumers of any product tend to go for image rather than wordy descriptions, it is certainly worth the investment of having key information translated, and/or perhaps having a video made, by your own students, which delivers the message in target languages. However, it is important to know when, and to what extent, to translate your information; in some countries such as Korea, 'Englishness' is a commonly held aspiration and translation may detract from the status of the product.

One final element involved in marketing overseas is working with an interpreter. This can be challenging and it demands practice, but it can be highly effective with proper preparation. The home market generally understands what independent schooling is about; that assumption cannot be made in overseas marketing. A clear message delivered with authority, humour and empathy, backed up by vibrant promotional materials, generally hits the mark.

Chapter 11

The vital importance of the admissions department

Admissions is another area in which day and boarding schools have similar priorities but also important differences of emphasis. The first writer is a Head; the second, a registrar.

Day schools

Kevin Fear

In many respects the work of the admissions department is the most important that any school does. Without the recruitment of pupils each year, the school quite simply cannot operate: thus the consequences of the admissions process going badly wrong are critical. The continuing existence of an independent school depends completely on maintaining its pupil numbers and the admissions department is the guardian of this vital task. The careful nurturing of each prospective enquirer is critical in determining whether a parent chooses you or one of your competitors.

What then, as a Head, do I hope to get from a well-run admissions department? Any good school depends on relationships, the key one being between pupil, parent and school – and this relationship starts at the very first moment that an enquiry is made. We have all phoned schools, only to be put on hold – or worse still to find no-one answering the phone at all – so having someone whose role it is to both be there and to deal with that initial enquiry is a key requirement.

Many people contacting independent schools are first-time buyers, and they are understandably a little intimidated by the reputation of our schools and our often imposing buildings. A friendly, helpful approach is therefore so important. How much more friendly it is to be told the name of the person you have rung, rather than have the impersonal name of the school repeated to you when you first ring them up.

This relationship with the person in charge of admissions then develops through many stages. Generally speaking, a prospectus will be sent out and a visit arranged. Here too the admissions department can ensure that people arrive at the Head's door in a good mood, by ensuring that they have a parking space and that the receptionist has been warned to expect them. It is even better if we have already found out a little about the prospective pupil, so that the tour can be tailored to their interest, and as Head you can make sure that you cover their areas of interest in your discussion with them. The admissions team can also ensure that you have a tour guide ready when the visitors arrive, and that the guide too has been briefed on the family that s/he is showing around.

As a Head I feel that it is vital that we keep notes of our meeting with prospective parents and that these are then recorded on our database. Doing so means that when I come to meet the parents and prospective pupil again, I can be briefed on what we have previously spoken about – and more importantly what information they have shared with us all. The recording of all of this information means that you can ensure that this whole process is kept personal. Given what an independent education costs, this level of personal service is extremely important.

The database of the admissions office is a vital tool for the Head. In my own school we are able to analyse week-by-week our current situation in respect of the number of enquiries or applications compared with previous years. This means that I am able to keep my governors fully informed of the likely position later in the year – which in turn means that we can plan staffing and resources at an early stage, rather than waiting until final numbers become clearer at the time of the entrance examination.

The data stored on this database is useful in many ways. Not only does it enable us to send reminders about the open day and entrance exam dates, but it also enables us to do some follow-up research on those who have enquired, but who then do not go on to apply. We also seek telephone feedback after an open day, so that we can inform the planning for the next one: this too really does enable the senior management team to reflect on the quality of our events and to ensure that they are always developing.

The quality of data that the admissions department provides is used to drive so many different decisions. It enables me to have an up-to-date picture of how many are applying for bursaries: this is useful because it is important to keep abreast, not only of the total number of people sitting the entrance exam, but also the proportion of them who are likely to be full fee-payers.

Once again, early warning of any differences from the norm helps to inform our planning with respect to staffing for future years. If we are likely to have a significant variation in numbers, one way or another, it means that we can plan the staffing accordingly. Thus, in more difficult economic times you might be able to avoid replacing a retiring teacher, and knowing this at an early stage in the year, through having good comparative data, means that you can plan well in advance. You cannot decide to expand the teaching staff overnight: governors need to be consulted, and finance must be found. Recruiting takes time, and it is easier to carry it out at certain times of the year – so knowing an accurate picture of your numbers helps here, too.

All this data is fine, but at its heart admissions is a sales process. The more your admissions staff can get to know the potential parents, the better. We work hard to personalise this experience; to encourage people to ring us with their queries; and to make the process less daunting. So the admissions team ensures that enquirers are invited to concerts and similar school events, and it provides me with good luck cards to send to all our applicants just prior to the examination.

The admissions department also organises our open days. The team helps me to welcome everyone into the school, and I often get a helpful word in my ear bringing information about the person approaching me. Never undervalue the importance of treating each person as an individual and learning something about them. The admission team shows our senior pupils how best to record the details of all those who attend, so that we can follow them up in the future.

Why? Because follow-up work is extremely important. Thus, when a prospectus has been sent and a visit *not* arranged, we seek to get back in touch with prospective parents to see if we can help further – and this often prompts them to book their visit. Similarly, we ring people shortly before the exam to ensure that they have every opportunity to sign up. As Head I am very aware of the value of this work: many people who come to see me comment on the friendly welcome that they have received throughout the whole process.

The admissions team also plays a very important role in liaising with primary schools. It ensures that their Heads and other key staff are invited to major school events and it also undertakes visits to their schools. It makes all the arrangements for a taster day for their pupils. In this respect, too, it becomes very much the public face of the school. I see our admissions department as the 'Director of First Impressions': it is thus vital that its members portray the school as the Head would wish. Conversely, it is important that the Head works with them to agree on the key messages that should be conveyed about the school at all times. The professionalism of the admissions department is essential but so too is the approachable, friendly smile.

I also know that in a good admissions department, people take each prospective parent to be individually important. If financial reasons rule someone out late on in the day, it is often bitterly disappointing to the admissions staff if they have formed a strong bond with such families.

In their role as 'Director of First Impressions' it is really important to me as a Head that the admissions department lives and breathes the qualities that we seek to convey as a school. Thus, the Head must play his/her part in ensuring that admissions staff know what the latest key messages are; s/he must support them by thanking all those involved in welcoming people to the school day after day, by passing on the positive feedback that their work generates and by being prepared to listen to what they have to say about visitors' perceptions of the school.

Rather than recounting to the Head what they have heard about the school outside in the community, parents are often much more prepared to open up to the admissions department during one of their many conversations with one of its members. Thus the latter become a rich source of information about the many and varied perceptions of the school held by those who engage with it.

But this is a two-way process: admission staff are also extremely well-placed to help the Head convey the key messages that the school wants prospective parents to hear. Thus, it is useful if they can be kept fully informed about the achievements of the school; the press coverage; the sporting results; even the difficult problems that arise from time to time – all in the interest of ensuring that such information can be passed on positively to prospective parents.

Thus, in so many ways, whereas the Head's PA is there to help the Head in his other daily work, the role of the admissions department is to become the Head's voice to the outside world. It is not practical for the Head to answer every incoming enquiry but, with a good admissions department, you can ensure that people are warmly welcomed, fully informed and then skilfully looked after – so that by the time they come to join the school community they feel very much a part of it.

Boarding schools

Charlie Bostock

Recruiting clients for the school in the form of registered and deposit-paid prospective pupils is more of a minefield for the boarding registrar than some people might anticipate. Whilst recruitment is manifestly the central activity, there is a host of other relevant variables to consider – as we shall see.

To a large degree the role is one that relies on relationships. These may be much more enduring than merely for the short-term: the admissions officer or registrar may well be both the first voice and the first face of the school, in a relationship that many schools (especially boarding schools, although increasingly day schools too) now seek to develop for life. Attracting the pupils to fill their rolls and the parents to pay their children's fees for the coming year is only the first stage of the story. Current and former parents and alumni alike will become the focus of the appeals to finance the capital projects of the future. In due course, today's school pupils may well be one of its future generations of prospective parents. A lost prospective pupil is thus potentially far more of a loss to the school than just a place unfilled at a particular time.

The business of ensuring that families come through the door relies on a series of relationships that fall under the marketing department's aegis. This too underlines the importance of the admissions department within the school as a whole, and means that the Head and registrar must act in concert – and that the messages that each gives out must be agreed, coordinated and consistently articulated to every constituency.

What are these key constituencies? Given that word of mouth recommendations are not easy to co-ordinate or control (although one enterprising school challenged its parental body to send out postcards to recruit to an open day!), the key architects of opinion who can be approached are the Heads of feeder schools. Cultivating and appreciating prep school Heads is an essential – and pleasurable – task for any boarding school admissions department: a good relationship with this constituency helps to ensure that the right pupils are recommended, and that an honest conversation between schools about potential and actual candidates is maintained over a sizeable period of time.

With growing demands for pre-testing at 11+ by senior schools, the complexities of scholarships that often differ from school to school, and the varying nature and reality of required Common Entrance pass marks of senior schools, there is plenty of administrative detail (as well as statements of broad ethos) that needs to be conveyed to feeder schools. The registrar often has to take initiatives, and offer some fine judgements, when communicating the school's policy and practice over entrance exams – especially in respect of individual candidates.

This work needs to be proactive in the main, and it may sometimes require an evangelical zeal to ensure that a strong and clear message is communicated. But on other occasions relationships with feeder schools may need to be reactive and more discreet: they may require quick thinking and a level head – for example when an exam candidate has been (from the prep school's point of view) unexpectedly turned down. The better the relationship and communication with the feeder school in the good times, through regular contact on the part of the registrar, the easier it is to handle the trickier issues when they periodically crop up, and to ensure that misunderstandings are minimised and good relationships maintained.

This relationship management is also a vital element in the school's dealings with its prospective families. The attention paid to detail in answering questions about the particular needs and interests of a prospective pupil will reap great dividends. But here too, a growing relationship with a prospective family can generate difficulties if (say) the eldest child is not made an offer. Empathetic counselling skills prove invaluable in managing a disappointed family; after all, the child may still be on the waiting list, or the family may yet have younger children who are more likely to sail through the exam, if and when their turn comes to take it.

There are times too when admitting a particular pupil may be seen as politically expedient (for example, if the parents have shown an interest in the work of the development office) but educationally highly risky. Admitting a child for the wrong reasons is *never* advisable: there are few more damaging and miserable situations for any child than struggling along in a school whose academic pace is far too demanding.

Moreover, in such cases when s/he inevitably fails to match the achievements of others, the school is invariably (and rightly) blamed. Furthermore, in a culture where anti-discrimination legislation makes its own demands, the registrar's policies and actions in respect of the candidate field as a whole must be able to stand up to legal scrutiny. Is there an admissions policy? How is it managed? Has it been even and fairly administered? What feedback is available to unsuccessful candidates?

If the winning or losing of a place is one of the main potential sources of friction in a registrar's relationship with prospective candidates and their schools, the other – at least, in a large or physically dispersed and federated boarding school – is the parents' choice of house.

This highlights the importance of the registrar's relationship with a third constituency: housemasters and housemistresses. The successful word of mouth recommendation that might help to deliver 100 candidates to the school might also unhelpfully (from the school's point of view) deliver them unevenly across the houses available. Registrars must sometimes say "no" – and then prospective parents must trust their recommendation about an alternative house. However, the more discerning ones will do so whilst knowing that the school's interest (in having *all* its houses filled) may well be rather different from their own (in securing a place for their child in the 'best' house available). In such circumstances a good registrar needs, as far as possible, to act even-handedly in the interests of both school and family.

In such 'decentralised' schools, it is up to the house and its staff to sell themselves to prospective parents, but if an independent-minded houseparent seeks to fill his/her own lists to an extent that prejudices the school's marketing effort as a whole, the registrar needs to step in and arbitrate. S/he also needs a wary eye to ensure that, overall, the house lists are coordinated, so that there is a clear and up-to-date record of who hopes to end up where. Ideally the registrar will be enough of an IT guru to oversee the effective storage and retrieval of information from a database and to present it handily via spreadsheets.

Houseparents who guard their lists jealously, but then fail to take any initiative on following up long-standing registered families, need either to be spurred into action themselves or persuaded to let the registrar do it for them. No Head wants to face a governing body in June with the admission that the 120 expected firm candidates at Common Entrance has turned out to be only 90, because nobody had thought to check that parents who registered many years ago were still interested.

There are benefits for a house itself in this common sense of endeavour and collaboration, too: it can be appropriately recommended to parents by the admissions department and places subsequently filled. A mutually cooperative approach also enables the registrar to support a houseparent in the annual round of budget bids, or in pushing for physical improvements to a house so that it can be more easily filled in the future.

Meanwhile even if the registrar has a personable manner, appropriate empathy, legal expertise and high level of IT competence to tackle all the issues already mentioned, his or her skills as a soothsayer and reader of the stars will be regularly drawn on in other ways. Governors, trustees, bursars, Heads and the SMT all seek regular estimates and projections of the numbers next term, next year, next decade... Whatever it is, the registrar is expected to know it, or to read it in the tea leaves.

There is an element of science in tracking demographic and sociological trends; of monitoring key ISC and BSA statistics through the year and from year to year. It's the registrar who needs to determine which idiosyncratic variables to monitor across the annual admission cycle, thus enabling the annual average percentage fall-out to be tracked so that the overbooked places are sufficient to fill the beds available. But which tea leaves would have predicted a modest rise in senior boarding numbers in an economy that is going through its worse crisis for a generation? And how will it be next year?

The element of science is thus balanced by elements of some dark art. It is surely a different type of tea leaf that predicts which house will deliver the unexpected space (through a family dropping out), so that the growing frustration of a family still languishing on a 'general list' as Common Entrance looms can be pacified.

Predicting future numbers accurately requires absolute honesty from parents, but in reality the world is rarely ideal. In the absence of such honesty, if it *were* ideal, there would be scope for greater cooperation between registrars in different schools over their lists in advance. However, such action might potentially be seen as anti-competitive and anyway it would still leave registrars none the wiser as to which way a family might jump.

Thus legal protocols too are an inevitable part of all facets of the admissions process. Their importance is highlighted at the stage where parents formally accept the offer. The registrar must be conversant with that most turgid of documents, the *Terms and Conditions*. The elegant simplicity of a term's fees in lieu of notice affords scope for significant brinkmanship at the start of a summer term, where a rushed round of changed minds affects prospective rolls. Moreover, likely as not the registrar becomes the bearer of the news of FILON (fees in lieu of notice) that may not have been entirely understood or appreciated by parents, in spite of the clarity of communication that comes as standard from the school and registrar's office.

As a key interface with the school's prospective clients, the registrar is not only critical in the purveying of the ethos, values and character of the school but also an important market researcher in what parents may be seeking from it. S/he needs a clear insight into its workings in almost every conceivable aspect from EFL to exeats; airport pick ups to A levels; fencing to French; uniform to university entrance stats.

S/he must also have the sensitivity to monitor and judge impartially the school's key areas of potential strategic importance: the place of weekly or flexi-boarding; of exeats; of key activities; the timing of scholarships and open days, *etc*. Conveying such information to and from all interested parties must be fitted around all the work and visits in a busy school where colleagues and pupils may have little space or flexibility to spare.

Other diplomatic and organisational abilities are useful skills in the registrar's armoury, too. These include being capable of managing colleagues and the wider school community, when another open day or raft of scholarships are due, which require diverse support and immaculate planning. Whereas colleagues tend not to be paid for the help and support they provide, the same cannot be said for the overseas agents – but if we are ever tempted to undervalue them, we should remember that they are additional allies to the registrar in his/her mission to maintain or raise numbers and standards: they too represent a constituency to manage and educate, for the mutual benefit of both sides.

Meanwhile national politics has also impacted on the registrar's role – in the shape of both the UKBA and the Charity Commission. The visa letter, so long a standard document of many an admissions office, has now been replaced with a slick computer-generated individual Confirmation of Acceptance of Studies (CAS) reference number, whose validity seems poorly understood by some of the overseas agents and whose lifespan is limited because of changed requirements at the point when a pupil reaches the age of 18.

Meanwhile the laudable principles of the Charities Commission offer their own challenges to an admissions office – including the need to consider specific and separate advertising to increase access to the school of suitable bursary candidates.

Clear and efficient management systems are required for each element of the admissions office role. All that said, it's a wonderful job – not least for the variety of people you meet and the multi-faceted nature of the work itself.

Part Three

Chapter 12

Educational development: a foreword

Nigel Richardson

Remember yet another old story. The development director is talking to a very rich potential major donor (PMD) on the phone.

"I hope I can count on you to contribute to our campaign?"
"Sorry, but my wife/husband is very keen that I support their sheltered housing charity."

The director follows it up some time later with an email, and gets this response: 'Sorry, my local village needs a new community centre and I've just been approached to help.'
   Eventually, the Director goes to see the PMD:

"Can you possibly consider helping us now?"
"Sorry, I've been asked to sponsor a new university department."
"I see... (A pause.). It must be really hard, having so many calls on your generosity."
"No, not really: if I can say no to all of them, then I can say no to you, too."

But how do you make people say "yes"? Our chapters up to this point have dealt very largely with how to mould public opinion about your school; create new markets; increase a share of existing ones and retain the people who comprise them.
   The public relations process is (as we have seen) all about the communication of good news to key constituencies: not just in marketing, but also in educational development. This is, in turn, made possible through skilful friend-raising and fundraising.

A school's friends comprise many outlooks, backgrounds and walks of life. They are linked to it through many different roles. They include parents and pupils – but many more besides. Governors want to hear about the results that their investment of time is producing. So do former staff (a constituency sometimes neglected): in their day, they invested huge amounts of effort in the place where they worked, in some cases over a period of up to 40 years. Members of the local community who have grown up around the school; lived in its area; occasionally or regularly crossed its threshold to open days or special events, like to know what it is up to.

A number of schools have been the amazed but grateful recipients of a large legacy from a hitherto unknown and unrecognised former pupil, or even, in a few cases, from an equally unassuming member of the common room who had secretly played the stock market! This highlights one of the cardinal rules in this part of the book: that even an apparently mundane conversation at a school event may yield unexpected results in fundraising terms a lot later on. You just never know.

Why do friend-raising, and fundraising, matter – and why will they matter even more in the years to come? To answer this question one needs to look both backwards and forwards.

It is widely recognised that the economic crisis of 2007 marked the end of 50 or 60 years of assumptions about more or less permanent economic growth. During that half century, how did the schools fare in terms of strategic development? Here one needs to look at three key areas of spending: buildings, scholarships and bursaries, and the growth of the curriculum.

Buildings: in the decade of austerity and rationing after 1945, schools did not escape the everyday harshnesses of life. Money was very tight: during the exceptionally hard winter of 1947, an ESU scholar from the warm and comparatively affluent USA arrived late at night at a boarding house in one of our most famous schools to be told that the boys could have either heating in studies, or hot water for baths, each day – but not both. (It does not appear to have scarred him for life: he went on to be one of New England's leading Headmasters.)

In that austerity era many independent schools had no capital building projects at all. Those schools that did, often built on a shoestring: thin walls of basic brick; metal window frames; poor insulation. Some of those buildings have long since been replaced, but others remain – often unloved and out of keeping with better-looking structures around them, but a monument to a time when every penny counted (sounds familiar?).

Then, it is often said, from the later 1950s (to borrow Prime Minister Harold Macmillan's famous election phrase) we "never had it so good". Independent schools got themselves into a half-century competitive building 'war', as schools fought over their share of the market by trying to show parents who could build biggest and most lavishly: sports centres; theatres; ICT suites; design/technology facilities and ensuite boarding houses were the prime examples.

Those decades of the second half of the 20th century were punctuated occasionally by periods of economic downturn – for example, in the mid 1970s, when a number of schools turned huge and now-redundant sanatoria into girls' houses, and the late 1980s when pre-preps began to open in former boarding houses. However, the long-term trend in terms of buildings was distinctly onwards and upwards in every respect.

Scholarships and bursaries have a complex history. As they began to expand their buildings, schools also became more concerned to lose their elitist and aloof image. Many day schools also had to face up to the twin threats posed by the abolition of the Direct Grant (1976) and the loss of Assisted Places (1997). Their achievement in doing so should not be underestimated – although a look at a list of schools that were members of HMC half a century ago but have since dropped out, suggests that more went into decline (in relative or absolute terms) than people sometimes realise. Boarding schools began to compete more aggressively with each other in a numerically declining market.

Some schools of both types also came to believe that they had a unique opportunity to develop exceptional talent in areas such as music and sport. Thoughtful people, both within and outside the independent sector, became increasingly concerned about two issues: the gross inequalities within the education system as a whole, resulting from the failure of comprehensive schools to be the panacea that their supporters had hoped for, and the diminished opportunities for academic high-flyers from poorer backgrounds caused by the abolition of grammar schools. More recently, the sector has had to face the legal requirements of the Charities Act in respect of public benefit.

In practice, all these changes led to two things above all: a desire to increase the funding provision for scholarships and bursaries (especially at 11-plus and 13-plus), and to schools switching funds from no-strings-attached scholarships to means-tested bursaries. But, as any financially literate Head (and all bursars) know, these awards are fearsomely expensive to fund.

The third long-term development centres on the curriculum, both within the formal timetable and beyond it. We have hugely increased the range of subjects, subject combinations and co-curricular activities on offer, whilst at the same time reducing class sizes. This again, as any Head or bursar will know, has a huge cost that is often not fully understood by others. So does the spiralling ambition of ICT initiatives.

Critics of this expansion claim that we have been profligate or financially illiterate. Supporters point to the paramount need for a school to combat competition from rivals in both sectors – and to the great educational benefits of new subjects and activities. Many of us feel that at least some of the oft-derided 'ologies' offer genuine benefits; few of us would wish to return to the days when schools offered just a basic, limited range of A levels, and no opportunity for high-flying 15 and 16 year-olds to take (I)GCSE subjects early and then to study (for example) Arabic or Japanese.

Those of us old enough to have taught classes of 40 at O level on teaching practice know that, despite what some experts claim about the lack of hard evidence of the benefits of small classes, some children always get overlooked when teaching groups creep above (say) the middle to high 20s.

And so, up to 2007, the independent sector thrived in a growing economy: its buildings, staff, facilities and curriculum/co-curriculum grew out of all recognition. Many took pride in this fact, although the more pessimistic commentators point out that the overall proportion of children being educated within it at any one time remained remarkably static at around 7%, from which they deduce that the impact of fees rising vastly ahead of inflation was already taking its toll.

Now, as a result of economic downturn, we all know that we ignore the future at our peril. To recap from chapter 3, those who constitute our market face ever-greater calls on their income: via a mixture of tax rises; employees' contributions; healthcare charges and (not to be underestimated) escalating university tuition fees. We know that fee rises will now have to slow down (or even stop altogether), whichever political party is in power over future decades.

Simultaneously, it seems highly unlikely that two of the fastest increasing costs for schools in times past will significantly decline in the future. First, even if some regulation and inspection levels are reduced, a certain level is here to stay. This is inevitable, given that state education is one of the biggest calls on the public purse and must therefore be highly accountable to parliament. No party will let the independent sector be treated any differently in some respects from the sector that educates the other 93% of children. Politicians of *any* party don't like to let go of powers once they have acquired them. The nation has an over-riding pre-occupation with safe recruitment and health and safety – and a fear of the legal consequences of being tripped up in such matters. The best that the sector can probably hope for is that there will be a slowing down of the increase in monitoring mechanisms in the long run.

Secondly, schools will find it hard to cut their salary bills – unless they are prepared to put some of their recent hard-won advances at risk. Will some of the best teachers move to more affluent schools elsewhere – to those that are already recruiting the best new entrants? How will parents react to increased class sizes and fewer curriculum options?

Meanwhile how much will all schools be subject to *future* rises in employers' pension contributions and national insurance payments (and changes in VAT), as the UK struggles to scale down its deficit; maintain its foothold in the global market and cope with the ever-increasing dependency ratio of old people to those in productive work? All this suggests a radical slowing-down in how schools develop and grow. A generation of Heads and governors that was highly adept at expansion may well be succeeded by one required to retrench and downsize.

To all this bleak news, you might be tempted to add one more thing: the same parents who may be struggling to pay our fees will no longer be able to contribute even modest sums to fundraising appeals.

So is there any *good* news? It is too soon (summer 2010) to know exactly how far the fiscal changes introduced by the new government will impact on independent school recruitment. But effective work in educational development gives us the opportunity at least to off-set their effects, by giving us an additional income stream through fundraising. It makes good things possible.

As the newspaper rich lists continue to show, the rich seem to be getting richer, even under governments dedicated to the redistribution of wealth in the search for what they call a 'fairer society'. The global market also creates global fortunes, through areas such as entertainment, professional sport, ICT and biotechnology. Some of these fortunes are made by people who are still very young. Even though they still constitute a small minority of the population as a whole, a growing number of successful entrepreneurs recognise their good fortune: they want to plough something back; to engage in charitable pursuits.

It also seems likely that a proportion of the baby-boomer generation, born just after the 1939-45 war and regularly reminded in the press of how fortunate it has been, will wish to recognise that fact through its legacies (although it will want also to cushion the impact of the new austerity on its own grandchildren). But all these groups will also want to be assured that the money they give is well used; that they know how it is being spent; and that they keep some control of it. If they 'retire' young, having made their fortunes, they have the time to keep an eye on these issues too – of which more later.

The challenge for the schools lies in indentifying them; cultivating their friendship and then keeping them satisfied over time. It's never too early to begin this process: a school that is only 20 or 30 years old needs to start work on it, just as a centuries-old institution needs to update long-neglected lists of names, or database information.

All this requires cohesive planning, and a comprehensive *strategy* grounded in well-deployed resources. Our schools represent a spectrum

144

in this respect. In a few, there has never been much systematic consideration of the main issues – either because of little interest on the part of the governing body or the Head, or more likely because of a lack of time and resources. In some, there have been periods of intense activity in the past, often in the run-up and through a major appeal, but the effort has then been dissipated. I think of the new Head who discovered, on his arrival, that the records from the appeal of six years earlier had been dumped in a distant unused building and were being systematically eaten, or nested in, by grateful mice...

But I also think of another school that had a real slice of good fortune, although maybe its extent is evident only with the benefit of long-term hindsight. A 13 year-old boy entered it in 1931, and left for university in 1936. A polio victim, he was unable to fight in the war, so he joined the staff. At a time of acute staff shortages, and with those who remained being forced to combine many roles, one of his was to run the old boys' society – which he did even after his retirement from teaching in the mid-1970s until his death in 1987.

Others have been able to build on his work since, and the school prospers strikingly in fundraising terms. He was its corporate memory – and any school that has someone with a length of service to rival his, and that does not capitalise on that person's memory, is missing a vital trick. Friend-raising is a process to be measured in years, even decades, rather than days or weeks – but it is never too early to start, and we owe it to future generations.

And, in time, friend-raising leads to fundraising. It can be done on a variety of levels, as succeeding chapters will show. At the smaller end of the spectrum there is an annual fund to parents. It may yield relatively modest returns (five figures rather than six) in the first few years, but it can be a good precursor to a larger-scale appeal later on – getting potential large donors into the 'giving habit'. It is a good way to engage members of the common room; to get them used to the idea that they can play their part in winning hearts and minds, and that the development office is on their side. How? Because the comparatively modest scale of an annual fund's projects means that they can often be delivered quickly:

the idea gets round that fundraising makes a difference. Moreover, a fund on this scale doesn't mean taking on expensive full-time staff.

In the middle of the spectrum comes the full-blown campaign – something to be rolled out once in every generation of pupils going through. At the other end of it there is the rolling campaign and the permanent foundation, with an office perhaps employing several people. Whatever your level of operation, the legacy campaign and the telethon, described later, can be useful adjuncts. There may be 'quiet phases' along the way – another opportunity to consolidate the raising of friends, and maybe to tackle that difficult constituency of former pupils who do not remember their schooldays in the 1960s and 1970s with great affection, but who may be persuadable that things have changed.

What can, and what cannot, be learned from the USA? People often point to it as an example of all that we should aspire to, especially if they have visited the great boarding schools of New England, with their vast sports complexes, impressive libraries, and wide-ranging access schemes – a few of them even admitting pupils on a needs-blind basis.

In some ways they are right to point to best practice across the Pond: we might well be able to replicate some American schemes for year-representatives to stoke up corporate loyalty. But it will take time, and the British are also probably more resistant to being told by their erstwhile school contemporaries what they should do with their money. The culture of 'one generation giving to the next the opportunities which it has itself been given earlier' has been slower to embed itself here than many people once hoped – partly because in the UK the potential tax benefits are comparatively limited.

How do we capitalise on that group of seriously wealthy people, of varying ages, who wish to find worthwhile outlets for their success, but who wish to retain some control over the use of what they give? At one time, most appeals, especially for bursaries, centred around the building-up of a permanent endowment. Donors were expected to hand over their donations in a once-and-for-all gesture, or at most in a number of annual instalments.

More recently, however, there has been a growing trend towards what some people call 'venture philanthropy'. Donors agree to provide funding for a specific project (for example, one bursary for one pupil for seven years from 11-plus), after which they will review whether or not to renew it in respect of another pupil. In some cases the donor knows the identity of the pupil, but not always.

This situation seems to have great potential. For the school, it helps towards its charitable intent (but only if it communicates regularly and skilfully with the donor, perhaps through an annual news bulletin after the entrance exam). For the donor, it enables control to be kept of the fruits of his or her generosity.

Meanwhile, as our own tax system has moved away from an emphasis on four- and seven-year covenants; as the concept of regular but one-off appeals has diminished; and as the rolling campaign has become more of the norm; the role of the development director has changed. It is now a more ongoing, long-term one – although until there are enough high-calibre candidates for the rapidly increasing number of jobs on offer, many experienced fundraisers will be in a seller's market.

Their efforts and status need to be better recognised rather than taken for granted, or they will continue to move regularly from one school or university to another, sometimes through the efforts of professional head-hunters. At the same time there will be an increased emphasis on the accountability of the development office, with regular oversight by governors: cohesive effort and good communication between governors, the Head and the development office is very important, especially where a school has a permanent foundation.

All these things represent a formidable but exciting challenge for an ambitious school. But in a rapidly changing world, some things remain certain and constant: momentum matters; people like to be associated with success; they like to feel that their contribution has made a difference. Read on to see the detailed ways in which we can capitalise on their positive instincts – and their generosity.

Chapter 13

The development office: an overview

Ian McLean

Since 1999 in the UK there has been a proliferation of schools establishing a development office – although in some cases, where the school has set up a separately constituted charitable foundation, it has been referred to as the foundation office. There are advantages of this foundation office model, especially when the trustees of the charity have taken passionate responsibility for fundraising and supported the overall development operation.

However, positive as this may be, it can send a clear message that, rightly or wrongly, the sole purpose of the office is fundraising for the school. In my opinion this contravenes the accurate description and benefit of development. Yes, it is correct that the end result of good development work is a sustained source of funding for the school, but development and a development office should be about so much more than this.

Development is the function of coordinating various inter-related activities to support the Head and governors in achieving the school's ongoing master plan of capital development and improvement, widening the access for students and generally securing the school's future. These activities can be grouped clearly into three linked functions:

• Alumni relations.
• Marketing and communications.
• Fundraising.

For many years it was common for schools to launch a fundraising appeal when they needed to embark on a new capital development. The tax system made it convenient. A fundraising firm was often engaged; as many members of the school community as possible were approached to make a donation; some contributed and the donation details were locked into a covenant; the banking system did the rest. Not many thank-yous, and little or no further contact with the donor! All in all, it was an expensive exercise. It was no wonder alumni, and the alumni association, became suspicious and kept their association separate from the school. We've all heard the comment from past years: "The school only contacted us when they needed our money!"

In the meantime schools elsewhere in the USA, Canada and Australia had moved towards the development model of establishing ongoing relations with former students; becoming directly aligned to the alumni association and respecting the wishes and interests of potential and existing donors – and in some cases their required time-frames. In some schools the alumni, parents and former parents have been brought under one 'association' umbrella, with activities supported or co-ordinated by the development office.

The result has been a closer school community, with a range of benefits providing students with better opportunities. Alumni have enjoyed closer links with their *alma mater* and have been flattered to be able to assist in whatever way they can: not simply donating money but also providing work experience and careers advice; supporting teaching staff as guest lecturers from industry and the professions; serving the school on the governing body; providing advice, expertise and much more. The development office now has a far wider function than merely raising funds. Successful fundraising will result if relationships are developed, and if the school constituency is communicated with in the correct way, so that its supporters share in the school's vision.

Opinions vary as to precisely how close the link should be between marketing, PR/communications and development. I am not necessarily suggesting that the first two should be part of the role of the development office but there are obvious links and the three must be coordinated. In some schools, they may be merged roles. What is of paramount importance is that the respective development and marketing managers work together and that the admissions and development departments are closely aligned.

The importance of alumni relations can often be underestimated by the school's marketing and admissions staff, but having a former student who is well informed about his or her old school and promoting its strengths is in itself a powerful form of marketing. Hence, it is a key benefit of a good alumni relations programme.

In the UK in the coming years, I believe we will see a gradual change in the development office structure to one in which the office will be the hub for all of the school's external relations activity such as:

- Alumni relations, including parent and past parent activity; links with alumni clubs.
- Communications and marketing.
- Recruitment/admissions.
- Fundraising.
- Archives/museum.
- Special events.
- Commercial activity/lettings.

To be effective and more widely acceptable to the school community, the fundraising strategy must be directly linked to, and supportive of, the school's strategic master-plan. The fundraising strategy will vary amongst schools depending on their current needs, but generally, by providing a mix of opportunities for giving, it will build sustained fundraising results and a culture of giving amongst current families and former students. As this happens, the need for a capital campaign for a specific development will often present itself: such a campaign is then more likely to be successful and more cost effective if ongoing relationships have been developed and normal expectations about the positive reasons for a school to fundraise are in place.

The staffing levels and structure of a development office will vary greatly, depending on the maturity of the programme at each school; the extent of the alumni relations' activity; and the level of fundraising in the past. The administrative functions of database management, research and event management are essential to support a development director whose focus will ultimately be with nurturing key relationships. An alumni relations manager who is directly linked to the alumni association should work hand-in-hand with the director. As the fundraising programme matures, expanding the human resources to include additional fundraising personnel to manage the annual (fund) giving will improve overall income levels.

What works?

What works, and what doesn't? I have found that most schools approach their development in much the same way – but again, the detailed approach largely depends on the maturity of the programme. The most experienced development offices will adhere to the proven principles based on solid relationships, and my own experience confirms this. However, on many occasions the 'unexpected' produces results. I have seen and done things the right way and the wrong way and I constantly find that there are variations that provide wonderful new opportunities.

Having been development director at a number of highly regarded schools and in contact with many others, I have found that there are a number of things that are consistent amongst those schools that produce a sustained and growing development operation with good results.

- Having a respected, influential and committed group of volunteers leading the fundraising effort and taking ownership of its success has set a tone by which others take notice. Having this leadership group lead by example with its members' own gifts, has established a high standard of giving. In the same way, having governors totally committed to the development process and making leadership gifts has made it much more acceptable for other major prospects to support the school.
- Those schools that have had a total commitment from the Head stand out as having successful programmes, especially when the Head, director of development, development chairman and chairman of governors are working closely as a unit.
- Having real and visionary needs that are shared by all concerned

151

within the school gives the development programme a proper focus and helps to raise everyone's sights as to what is possible.

- Securing the moral and tangible support of the common room and receiving early donations from members of the school management have added much to the strength of the development programme. Maintaining ongoing communication with the staff and showing clearly how fundraising provides direct benefits to their work, helps to promote and expand the development operation.

- In the UK (more so than in Australia and the United States), I have found that the development director must take personal responsibility for the cultivation of major prospects. Volunteers have not been accustomed to making approaches at this level: they still feel uncomfortable at the thought. In the US and Australia the volunteer network is stronger and there has been a greater acceptance by volunteers that their role is vital. Having personal contact with major prospects and an ongoing relationship with donors has been the most enjoyable aspect of my time in development.

- One of the major aspects of a successful programme has been the correlation between the extent of the alumni relations' activity and the success of fundraising. Placing a high level of importance on alumni relations in the development process and dedicating the staff and resources to it is essential: those schools that have given this a low priority have suffered as a result. I have enjoyed tremendous success by cultivating close relationships with those in the over 60s age group.

- At an early stage I learned the importance of identifying the right person to take the leadership role for the legacy bequest programme. Once again, a person of respect and influence who has committed at a personal level has made the growth of bequest fundraising much more effective.

- Those schools that have supported the concept of annual giving as the basis for all fundraising have seen the benefits in more ways than just a steady stream of income. Annual giving identifies major donors, creates a culture of asking, as well as a culture of giving, within the school community and provides a vehicle for the school to promote its needs to a wide audience. The schools that have rejected annual giving are prone to always being 'on the back foot'.

- 'You have to spend money to make it.' This applies to a high degree in development work: I have seen schools where very limited resources are made available for the development function and yet there have been unrealistic expectations placed on the office. A fully integrated development operation covers a broad range of activity and success will be quicker and sustained with an up-to-date database, appropriate software, sufficient staffing levels, good communications and quality promotional material and budget.

- Having the development office in a prominent and welcoming location sends a message that the school places a great deal of importance on the development function. I have always tried to create an office where visitors, former pupils in particular and staff feel comfortable, knowing they can call in at any time and will be made to feel welcome. Providing archival or memorabilia pieces in a professionally displayed way has helped them feel warm and attached, and wanting to help where they can. The office that is small, uninviting and perhaps located 'out at the back' does nothing to encourage support.

What doesn't work?

By contrast less successful, or failed, programmes tend to show one or more of the following characteristics:

- A hurried, unplanned and desperate approach to fundraising with short-term thinking. Aligned to this is the pressing need for funds, arising from the poor financial performance of the school. Having no compelling case for support to provide a purpose for fundraising is a common reason why development offices under-perform.

- An expectation that immediate results will come once a development director is appointed, with no acceptance of the integrated development process. Development is a long-term and permanent process, and it takes time to build.

THE DEVELOPMENT OFFICE: AN OVERVIEW

- A low regard by a school for the importance of alumni relations. Such schools often still struggle to counter the argument of 'you only contact us when you want money!'
- Governors not believing that they have an important role to play in the development process, and therefore not placing any relevance on setting a leadership example. Their contacts and influence are often underestimated.
- The appointment of the wrong people as trustees or development council members. There is no surprise in such situations when leadership gifts are not forthcoming.
- Heads feeling they are too busy to be involved in development, and believing that such work is simply the role of the development director. In schools where this situation is the norm, there will always be cracks appearing in the programme.
- A school expecting that former pupils will give, simply because they are former pupils; that big gifts will be forthcoming without cultivation of, and close involvement with, major prospects; where writing letters asking for major gifts rather than using a face-to-face approach is the *modus operandi*. These are all proven recipes for failure.
- A school ignoring good consultancy advice; not providing sufficient resources for the development office and ignoring the basic principle of seeking major gifts: this sort of school has failed in 'getting the right person, to ask the right person, for the right amount of money, for the right reason, at the right time'.
- A school appointing the wrong person as development director and then expecting miracles.

Over the years, I have heard the following or similar comments in different schools:

"Our old boys are not good givers."
"We don't have a wealthy group of former pupils."
"Former pupils of our school are different from everyone else."
"We've tried that reunion a few years ago and it didn't work."

And many more such observations! In general, most schools in our western culture, and the people associated with them, are very similar. For that reason, the fundamentals of successful fundraising and development in general remain consistent.

In summary, as a development director, if I had known 20 years ago what I know now about managing development office activities, when starting out I would have:

- Got out more and personally asked for support, rather than expecting volunteers to do it.
- Aligned myself and the office even more closely to the alumni association and its committee.
- Started an annual giving programme immediately.
- Been more active in promoting bequests.
- Thought more in terms of the donor's interests and not the school's.
- Maintained an ongoing 'consultancy' with experienced development directors.
- Involved and informed the common room as much as possible about development activities.
- Expected the unexpected. Big results come when you are least expecting it and the predictable major donation may simply never come.
- Always created and worked with an enthusiastic and respected group of volunteers as a development council.

I have learned:

- Not to worry about the sceptics who knock the development programme – just keep going! Not everyone wants to support their school, but the key to development work is finding those who do.
- To respect that governors give enormously of their time, but also to encourage them to take some ownership of fundraising and set example to others.
- To make sure the Head enjoys development work and its success.

The late Michael Mavor, former great Headmaster of Gordonstoun,

Rugby and Loretto, encouraged his pupils and staff to enjoy the feeling of 'exhaustive achievement'. In development work, that feeling is very rewarding!

Chapter 14

Alumni relations

Catherine Reeve

Although the goodwill and value generated from a receptive and supportive alumni body can only be measured over time, a successful development office must have the relationship with former pupils at the forefront of its thinking and activities. Our work would not be possible without them. Development is all about people: building relationships; making connections; bringing people together after many years apart; making the occasion both personal and emotional; recognising the spirit of a community; directing the natural energy and enthusiasm and through all of this clearly demonstrating why the school is worthy of support.

One of the interesting tasks for a development director is working out how to keep the future continuous with the past; and keeping the memories of alumni alive when they re-trace their school-day steps. It can be a difficult concept for a common room to grasp that former pupils actually *like* to return to their *alma mater*. It is understandable that the focus of teachers is very much on the present – and to a certain extent the future – whereas the development role is often to bring the past, as realistically as possible, closer to the present and the future.

This can be a delicate balance at times and needs constant attention, empathy and understanding. Sometimes (for example, when a school is facing difficult economic times) it is necessary to make small changes in order for more important things to stay the same, and for their continuing existence to be guaranteed. This is certainly a feature of development and it is vital that these changes are communicated in a way that encourages a feeling of belonging.

It is this sense of belonging to a family, a community or a shared heritage, that requires nurturing; at certain times throughout their lives an alumnus or an alumna is inevitably going to reflect on the values learnt at school; values that often remain with them for a lifetime. This is why the development office plays such a crucial role in improving and keeping contact with alumni and ensuring that the relationship continues to go from strength to strength.

It is the responsibility of the development office to take on a lifetime commitment (on behalf of the school) to each former pupil. This takes time, effort and perseverance – as with a marriage, or any long-term relationship. From the day that they leave the school, alumni will be asked regularly for support from many other charitable organisations – including, increasingly, universities – so it is vital that the benefits of the development office are recognised and appreciated whilst still at school.

This also means that it is as important to engage with *current* pupils as with alumni, because they all hold the keys to the future. We are all in the business of promoting the benefits of a good education and asserting that it lasts forever. If we believe this, the opportunity to have a lifelong relationship with each pupil becomes a real possibility. An appropriate slogan for the development office might well read: 'School is for life.' After all, it is the lifetime experience that will prove invaluable – but it also challenges you to connect with individuals in effective, but changing, ways at the various different stages throughout their lives.

Once you have recognised that alumni relations are a lifetime commitment, it is easier to accept that there is a considerable amount of planning involved in delivering results. However, the road to success is through a simple structured approach that concentrates on the basic principles of improving relationships through good communication, professionally managed events and demonstrating clearly the tangible benefits of remaining in touch with the school. There are five key areas to concentrate on in respect of this work.

Building and maintaining relationships
The key to any successful business relationship is to collate every relevant piece of information to give you a thorough understanding and knowledge of your target market. It is no different with alumni: you must, crucially, listen to their views; inspire them with what the school is trying to achieve; receive feedback positively (even when it is critical) and gradually begin to exceed their expectations.

How much do they care about the school? If they care about it passionately, they are more likely to want to support it in some way, or will begin to warm to the idea of playing a more serious role in its future prosperity. Find out what is important to them: it will also be important to others. Every conversation has the potential to open another door. In most cases people are flattered to be asked for advice, so at the end of a discussion it is always worthwhile asking for a personal referral to another contemporary.

Despite the technology of the 21st century, word of mouth is still one of development's most frequently used tools, and peer-to-peer conversation is extremely powerful. There is no doubt that people still respect and respond more to personal contact – whether this is done face to face in a meeting, on the telephone, or in a simple handwritten letter. The personal touch serves as a clear signal that you are prepared to dedicate time and effort to the relationship and it would be unusual for it not to be appreciated.

In many respects we are at a distinct advantage in that the alumni all have one thing in common: they attended our school. Most of them are naturally responsive to the institution where they spent their formative years – although in varying degrees. It is relatively easy to open up a conversation when you can identify with particular aspects of somebody else's life.

Meanwhile, although this chapter deals primarily with alumni relations, it should not be forgotten that former parents too are closely connected to former pupils. This fact is worth remembering in the general objective of relationship building. Parents make a huge commitment in their choice of a school, and many will still feel attached in some way after their offspring have left – whether it is through close associations with members of staff; other parents; through memories of financial help received; of pastoral care or just because of the fact that they cherished the time spent there over the years. Building relationships alongside the main body of the alumni produces a ripple effect similar to a Mexican wave and it strengthens the whole development experience.

We are all aware that success breeds success. It follows from this that alumni like to be associated with a flourishing school and are therefore more likely to give support to a thriving institution than a failing one. Has the school helped them to be successful in their career? Are their later achievements celebrated and publicised?

It goes almost without saying that prospective parents are another constituency that likes to see its chosen school succeeding and prospering, and this view is only enhanced with an active and prominent alumni body. Everybody likes to feel part of a successful operation: to bathe in a certain amount of reflected glory. It is important that this message is communicated right across the board to prospective parents, current parents, pupils, former pupils and former parents, so that everyone is involved in past and present success, with the realisation of the potential for even greater achievements in the years to come.

One of the many reasons for establishing excellent working relationships with alumni is that the process identifies those who want to help and be influential in the future prosperity of the school. Their presence, and their engagement with the development office, will gradually help their peers to reflect on the impact that the school had on them and to inspire them to be supportive in whatever way they can.

The aim must be to keep both alumni and parents connected to the school that helped shape their lives. It is often said that in times of difficulty we rally to those organisations that mean the most to us. This is why it is so crucial to be working everyday at the relationship with your alumni: their support demonstrates a belief in the school and emphasises the importance of its mission in securing a valuable education for future generations.

Alumni events
'It was a moving step back in time for the majority of us there, but also an occasion when we were able to see that the school's future is bright.' This quote, from a thank-you letter after a former pupil event, summarises perfectly why these occasions are so important to alumni. Obviously the main objective of holding events and reunions is to re-unite the alumni body after many years apart, in a location and atmosphere that will stimulate their original attachment.

The emotions surrounding this experience very often lead to a strong re-connection with the school, almost like a reaffirmation of marriage vows.

In many schools, the majority of former pupils do not return to their school for a decade or two, and for many it is even longer. Life intervenes; there are numerous distractions, one after the other, in the form of university, career progression, family commitments, location and a general reluctance to be seen to be returning too soon. Without doubt, it is one of the most rewarding sights to see former pupils picking up a conversation after 50 years, almost as if the years have not intervened at all.

A bold and varied events' programme will provide the backbone to a development office too, as well as a real sense of confidence to the basis on which to build all fundraising endeavours. Each occasion must have a particular focus that will draw different individuals back into the fold, and will appeal to different age groups; such occasions can be subject based, as in art, music or sport; centred around a personality (a famous alumnus/a, an inspirational teacher or a former notable Head); an anniversary or centenary; a year group; an unusual venue or a professional gathering offering networking opportunities ... the list is endless.

The point is that you offer a selection of occasions that will appeal to a wide audience. These events are so important for such a wide variety of reasons: not only do they bring people together and reunite them with memories and places that helped shape their future life, but they give the school the opportunity to show that the place they loved is still a vibrant, successful community.

Every event is another opportunity to build on the general relationship; there will always be newcomers who will bring news of others and there will be regular attendees whose presence is a testimony to their continuing loyalty and support for the school that requires constant nurturing.

Aside from the general feeling of goodwill that events and reunions can produce is the positive evidence from increased attendance figures to the revelation that even a refusal of an invitation is positive. I have lost count of how many times I have been told by alumni in a RSVP that they are very disappointed not to be able to attend an event but are still asking me to keep them on the invitation list for the next one. So a negative response is not necessarily negative, as it has the effect of increasing the general awareness amongst the alumni body of what is happening at the school and underlining again a blossoming community. Numbers at events can vary, and although smaller numbers might initially appear disappointing, there is also a lot to be gained from an intimate gathering – and in many ways the information revealed at such events is more valuable.

The overall satisfaction of an event is often measured by how many other contemporaries are attending and which former members of staff are present; never underestimate the value of former members of staff, (including former Heads), as many of these people will have had a huge influence on the lives of the alumni. It is often overlooked that these occasions offer the very real possibility of making *new* friends too amongst peers, and indeed other year groups, as well as meeting up with old friends.

This fact was brought home to me at a drinks reception for new leavers, where it was apparent that the former pattern of social interaction had changed in only six months, and it was noticeable that new friendships were made. There is no doubt that for the young and the old alumni events help to keep former pupils engaged and connected to their *alma mater*.

Database management

The importance of managing the database to support the entire development office operation is often underestimated. However, this can be such a valuable resource – always provided, of course, that the information is accurate. Collecting good data must always be one of the prime objectives. Once the development office has been set up, it is relatively easy to transfer information about new leavers on to a database each year, and this should form part of good practice. However, the real work that will need to be done lies in improving the details about pupils who left the school *before* the advent of the development office.

In order to be effective, it is vital to have basic information about each individual: contact details; university and subject choice; career; marriage; interests at school; how frequently they communicate with the school and whether they have made a donation. There are many ways to do this: contact and feedback forms on the website and in newsletters or magazines; daily telephone conversations in the office; a telephone campaign; alumni events; research on the internet and archive information.

First impressions are important when getting in touch with alumni after many years and it is essential that any contact and new information has been recorded, so that the details can be relied on in the future and used to benefit both the school and the individual.

Communication

Good communication is a prerequisite at all levels in raising the profile of the school, the development office, and what it is together they are aiming to achieve: in other words, the overall mission statement. Strategic messages need to be delivered effectively and accurately. It is difficult to over-communicate in these situations, although more communication leads to more work: more feedback; more accurate information and ultimately more understanding of the alumni.

If you are *not* communicating, that in itself means you are communicating badly. However it is also worth bearing in mind that unplanned or rushed communications can be sent out which fail completely to connect with the recipient.

It is remarkable how much good communication is appreciated; how correspondence will develop from it and ultimately how the first stage of involvement is achieved. It is also heartening to see that handwritten communication from the development office still plays a significant role in delivering a personal touch: something that has become so rare in our culture of email and mailshots, and which is particularly important for the older generation.

In today's market, we need to be able to communicate in so many different ways to connect successfully with all age groups: magazines; newsletters; e-newsletters; letters; telephone; website; DVDs and, of course, face-to-face. Clever communication is fundamental to any relationship and is an integral part of alumni relations.

Archives

The archives are a wonderful resource for the development office. They perform the very necessary function of bringing the past closer to the present for many alumni and they also provide a glimpse of the traditions and heritage of the school to the current generation. It is not always possible to hold events and reunions at the school, as its location may not be convenient for various practical reasons: in such circumstances it is essential to take along a part of the school with you.

A portable display from the archives enhances any occasion and makes it immediately poignant for the guests; these days it is nearly always possible to find a photograph of those attending from their time at school and this makes the event both special and personal for everyone. Copies of archive photographs can be sent out afterwards to the alumni, along with a photo of the recent occasion which ensures that the memory of the day is not forgotten. A well-structured archive department will prove to be a valuable link between the school and the alumni: it can make a huge contribution towards rekindling sentimental feelings about a place, and can provide a solid foundation to build on in the future.

Summary of results and benefits
The end result of building lasting relationships and communicating effectively is successful fundraising. There is a lot resting on alumni relations and therefore it is worth dedicating a significant amount of time to getting it right.

The steps to achieving this are numerous: engaging the alumni; maintaining the lifelong link; identifying potential supporters; cultivating the relationship and ensuring that educational fundraising is at the forefront of any communication. Over time, the close relationship and understanding between the school and the alumni will help to provide advocacy; promote the development programme and encourage the ongoing concept of giving and support for the school.

Another benefit of successful alumni relations is to see pupil numbers increasing because the alumni are sending their own children to be educated at the school. This is beneficial in two ways: the school has a healthy register of pupils and, from a development perspective, it means that the parents, as alumni, remain loyal and supportive towards *their* school rather than to a different one. It is for this reason that development must be seen to be educationally-driven, so that potential customers are not lost to another market.

Alumni are faced with many choices about which charities they choose to support. It is therefore incumbent on each school to be transparent with the monies raised and to ensure that donors are thanked often and recognised accordingly. The recent charity legislation has ensured that the role of the development office will be pivotal in helping schools meet their funding for bursaries. Although we have traditionally looked to alumni for help with new developments and capital projects, it is becoming increasingly obvious that they now consider bursaries, and the possibility of widening access to more pupils, to be cases very much worthy of their support as well.

Chapter 15

Relationship fundraising

Tony Bretherton

Philanthropic fundraising is *all* about people. The mantra taught to all new fundraising professionals is: people don't give to projects; they give to people with projects. Direct mail is less effective than a phone call invitation to give, and a phone call is much less effective than sitting down with someone over coffee and asking face-to-face. That's because people respond best to people and, in terms of fundraising, best to inspirational people.

This chapter will underline the importance of *people* in the process of fundraising. Processes matter, of course, and there are many other issues to attend to. Research; data accuracy; the link between fundraising projects and the school's strategic plan; communication systems; gift acknowledgement and thanking processes all matter. But a giving culture requires an asking culture, and the more meaningful gifts are given within the context of linkage, understanding, vision and trust.

Almost always the person giving a large gift must be effectively linked in to the life of the school, have a deep understanding of the value of the project, be strongly motivated, and committed to making a positive difference. All these things happen best when someone who embodies an inspirational spirit invites another person to join them on an adventure; shows them a doorway that leads to an experience that is personally rewarding and yet of significant benefit to others.

Relationship fundraising – indeed all effective philanthropic fundraising – is not about wielding an iron bar, somehow to extract the maximum amount of money from someone, and thereby to provide the greatest amount of pain possible; rather, it is about providing intelligent and caring people with opportunities to serve, to contribute, to build and to give.

It is an extraordinary privilege to be the one who opens the door, or the one responsible for what lies beyond. Major gifts usually come within the context of real, and often deep, human relationships, where understanding, trust, vision, motivation and deep belief are genuine – and lived out by those asking and those giving.

So what are some of the key guidelines to effective relationship fundraising? What processes help us to gain effective results? What are some of the considerations that will help us to make effective progress?

First, make sure the school has a good database. Relationships are all about people, but the human memory fails and people move on. Institutional memory and information about people is a vital resource and fundamental to what can be achieved long term.

Secondly, make sure you invest in effective research. Usually we know something about the people we meet, but seldom do we know enough. We need to know about their time at school, and what they have done in the world since leaving. Do they play golf, drink red wine, invest in the share market, own a yacht, belong to the parish vestry, enjoy keeping up with classmates? It takes time to learn about people, but experience shows that if we invest the time and energy, we gain the capacity to form better relationships and to raise far more money.

People often say 'no' six or more times before they say 'yes'. People usually make six or more small gifts before trusting you with a large gift. A legacy comes when there is a deeply felt love and respect for the institution, and that love and respect will have usually evolved because people took time to embody the school and its vision, its purpose, over many years.

Thirdly, ensure that there is an integrated advancement (development) programme, embedded for the long term. There was a time when the fundraiser was seen as a necessary evil: someone who came in to raise the money needed for a project and then left as soon as possible, to everyone's relief. That model is not a wise investment for a school. Best results will come from permanently embedding philanthropic activity within the school.

The typical overall programme would include an annual fund seeking small gifts every year from everyone; a major gift programme that develops relationships and involvement (with gaps between projects to mitigate benefactor fatigue), and a legacy programme that looks to the long-term development of the school. Legacy programmes have relationship building at their heart, and they require proper staffing and resourcing.

The more human contact and engagement we create, the more effective the 'ask', and the more likely a financial gift. It would be most effective if everyone was asked face-to-face every year for their gift to the annual giving programme, but that is simply not possible. So we use direct mail, telephone calling and then, for the few, and usually for significant gifts, we use our rarest and most valuable resource: time and human presence. Preferably between people who know one another.

Having identified the major prospects for a campaign or other major gifts project, a 'moves management' process is required. Some people don't like the terminology – but it represents a process that is at the very heart of relationship fundraising. Every time you identify someone whom you want to ask for money, there are four variables you need to attend to, and a five-step process that you are implementing in order to build the school for the future.

The four variables are wealth, linkage, knowledge and motivation. The process involves identification, assignment, cultivation, asking and stewardship. Overall it helps us manage relationships and understand what we are doing and why. Add genuine friendships and inspirational people, and you have the key ingredients that make a real difference.

We need to know how much money a prospect has, so that we don't embarrass them or ourselves by asking for too much (or too little). We need to know how well-linked into the school they are, and to take deliberate steps to increase the perceived level of linkage between the prospect and the school.

Similarly, we need to enhance their knowledge of what is proposed – the case for support – and how well motivated they are to support the project. Once we have enhanced linkage, project knowledge and motivation to support the funding of that project to the highest level possible, and once we have built a positive level of human rapport, we are ready to ask them for support.

In terms of process we *identify* the person because of their known wealth, or because they are part of our school family. They thereby become a prospect. They remain in the 'prospect pool' until they are *allocated* to a professional or volunteer fundraiser for concerted attention. No one can form relationships with an endless number of people at the same time. The University of Denver assigns 135 prospects to a full time professional major gifts officer, and cultivating that number of people is regarded as a full-time role. Other institutions allocate larger or smaller numbers, but the point is that there is a limit to how many people each individual can effectively cultivate.

Where a school has employed a single professional development director to manage fundraising, that person will also be running annual giving, a legacy programme and a database, as well as providing reports and encouragement to volunteers. S/he will do well also to relate to 50 major gift prospects, and s/he will probably only have time and energy to ask ten of those in any one year. If there is to be more asking, you must involve more people.

Next comes the *cultivation*, as each prospect is 'moved', dinner by dinner; meeting by meeting, worship service by worship service, briefing seminar by briefing seminar, special meeting with the principal by special meeting – from wherever they are in terms of linkage, project knowledge and motivation, to the point at which these key criteria are as developed as far as possible. Hence the term 'moves management'. Throughout the process, which may take up to 18 months, the relationship – between the person who will do the asking and the prospect to be asked – has been growing steadily. Trust and friendship and a sense of shared journey and challenge are established. Then the *ask* itself is made.

If there is a good relationship between prospect and asker, there will almost never be offence, awkwardness or disaster. It helps if you say something like: "You know a lot now about our new sports pavilion and I wonder if I may put a proposal to you whereby you might help support the project?" A "no" makes it clear that they are not ready to support the project.

However, many will say: "Yes, what's on your mind?" Or something like that. This leads to an invitation to support the project. There are a number of ways in which the 'ask' can be done, depending on the nature of the relationship – but it's always best face-to-face. As they say around the world, to get the right answer we need the right person asking the right person for the right amount of money at the right time for the right project in the right way.

There are just two key questions and they have often helped me to secure a gift. And there is just one rule that applies when asking both questions. First, always ask for a specific sum of money: "Would you feel able to invest £50,000 in this new concert hall?" Second, if they say "no", you can always then say something like: "I understand but, you know, we would really like you and your family to be able to be involved with us in this very special endeavour, so I wonder what would need to change in order for you to be able to participate?" Often this leads to a gift, be it for some other project or for some different amount of money.

The rule when using these two questions is this: in every case, and despite however you feel and whatever they do, they must speak next, after you ask either of these questions. Relationships need to be respectful and these questions are clear and honest, and do nothing to damage a good relationship, especially if we make certain to thank the person for considering the matter, whatever the outcome may be.

Stewardship is the last step in the process. Here we ensure that we maintain the relationship into the future. If there is a gift, we say "thank you" six times (in different ways over a period of time) and undertake all the many follow-up tasks. If there is not, we thank them for considering our proposal, and we try to leave the prospect feeling accepted, valued and positive about the school.

All of this is a process embedded within human activity, evolving unseen in the context of the relationship between those seeking funds and those being asked for the money.

So, how can we maximise income results? By having warm, effective relationships with those from whom we seek support, and by understanding and following the steps that must be integrated into each human interaction. Every such interaction is thus deliberate, intentional, and purposeful. Moreover, as we add inspirational leadership, so we increase gift numbers and gift size.

There are many specific aspects of human interactions to which we can pay attention, thereby enhancing fundraising outcomes. Everyone has their own list and the following is not exhaustive – but I offer it to start you thinking and to inspire you to pay attention to the people from whom you seek funds. They are not just prospects: each and every one is a person with dreams, hopes and aspirations.

- A donation can come anytime; an investment is part of a relationship. When we give a donation, it's often small and we don't tend to track how the money is used. An investment is altogether different, as we are making a more substantial commitment. Ask for an investment in the lives of children – not a donation to the school.
- If the gift really matters, there will be clear motivation for giving it. If you can understand what motivates a prospect to make a meaningful gift, you can build that into your 'ask'.
- Walk at their pace – take people seriously. Some prospects will ask for time out – or for a faster process, as they say "I want to know what you want me to do" before we feel ready to tell them. The potential benefactor calls the tune and we need to be flexible and responsive.
- Change the relationship, or change the person asking, and you can sometimes change the level of the gift. One person cannot get on perfectly or effectively with everyone. Sometimes there are very clear signals that person A is better to work with a particular prospect than person B. Put the prospect at the centre of what is being undertaken – not the process or personal pride.
- Trigger emotional connection before asking for a gift. If someone enjoys music and you seek support for a music building, make sure they enjoy a wonderful concert by your pupils before asking them for the gift.
- A quick 'yes' may mean that they could give more. If they seem to be very interested in the project, see if you can come up with ways of suggesting a higher amount: "Oh, and I should have mentioned that there are also some naming opportunities available with this project – would you like me to explain what's available?"
- If relevant, listen for the human pain before you try to sell or evoke

the new linkage, motivation, warm feelings. If you discover they were not thanked for their last gift, don't try to ignore that reality. Discuss it and be open about the school's failure to properly say 'thank you'. Only then can you move on to new opportunities.

- Ask for advice, but don't create false expectations. Involvement and engagement with the school and its key projects makes all the difference. "So what might you do or suggest?" is a good way in, but it is never appropriate to allow funders or a fundraising committee to begin to define a specific project. Ensure that the school knows what it wants – where and when and at what cost – and only then begin to involve fundraising volunteers and potential benefactors.

- Give them memories that will remain with them forever. I was privileged to take Frank McCourt, author of *Angela's Ashes*, down to Florida, USA, for a number of visits: as a result, eight residents of Florida flew to Ireland to discover the land of their forefathers.

    They spent a night in a farmhouse in deepest County Limerick and listened to *Riverdance* composer Bill Whelan entertaining on guitar. They will never forget that night. They returned to Florida and worked tirelessly for the University of Limerick, believing in a dream that they had experienced in a very deep and meaningful way.

- Find out what they yearn for and, where possible, help them to achieve it. Effective fundraising is not about driving people towards something they don't believe in. Rather, it is about opening doors and showing people what can be experienced by walking on through. In the end the goal is to help people do what they already deeply care about and want to achieve.

- Note whether they have children – and note if they don't. It sounds a little odd but the facts are indisputable: those without children (and without partners) are looking to do something with their estate that really matters. Those without children often leave their resources to their university or their school.

- Recover disasters with honesty, and make sure dreams are grounded in reality. Research shows that people lose faith in organisations that always 'spin' reality to show a perfect track record in all things. If you have three staff suspended for drug offences, it is better to acknowledge it, to report the lessons learned and actions taken to ensure it is less likely to happen again. People will be interested, and will connect more deeply with a school they perceive as being real and realistic. They are also more likely to decide that such a school is worthy of their financial support.

• People are in every case different. One size fits one. Each person is different and each personal ask is different. Remember that prospects are individuals – and while the project and case for support may be essentially the same, each person must be approached in a somewhat different, carefully considered and respectful manner.

• Listen, above all. It is implicit in some of the points above. Creative or deliberate listening is a great skill for development professionals to learn. Careful listening helps the prospect become a real person, as we learn about their hopes, aspirations, problems, families, challenges, successes and failures – providing us with knowledge we need for the 'ask' to be effective.

• Spend time with people who have influence and/or affluence. Those who have influence will lead you to people with the affluence necessary for you to be successful. You cannot be effective without these people. Without offending others, and within the context of valuing all members of the community, it is still necessary to chose carefully the relationships you invest time in. You can only do so much yourself.

• Think emotion, inspiration, belonging. An inspirational advocate can inspire connection, engagement and commitment. A gift can double as the individual becomes increasingly convinced that his or her financial support is necessary, wisely invested in the project, and highly valued. That this is their school, their project, that the outcomes are emotionally fulfilling.

• Think mystery, sensuality, intimacy. The sound of the orchestra, the challenge of teaching children to value others around them, the privilege of being one of the three people who can act at this level for the good of a community that we love... Making people feel special and needed and effective in achieving outcomes important to them: that is the task.

- Ask. It is obvious and fundamental but, so often, very difficult. But more often than not, it moves things forward. The worst thing that can happen is that someone says "no" – and that may be the first step towards an eventual "yes".

Chapter 16

Managing expectations

Jane Vines

The great challenge in managing expectations within your school begins with people's understanding of what development means and that it is *not* a euphemism for fundraising. So whose expectations are you trying to manage? In this chapter we shall address the expectations of the governors, staff, parents, alumni and pupils and share ideas on how to manage each constituency.

In most schools the expectation is that as soon as you open a development office, you will magically start to raise funds. However, although this is true in the medium and long term, if you simply relate it to fundraising, you will totally underestimate the power of a good development programme and what it can mean for your school.

Generating new income streams is a by-product of good development, and the overarching aim of the development office is to foster, in all those who care about the institution, a lifelong interest in sustaining its principles and securing its future. The office's first role is to reconnect your alumni with each other and with the school; secondly to create meaningful ways for alumni to engage with the school of today; thirdly to assist the school with strategic planning and finally to communicate the vision to the wider community.

If your community is nurtured, cultivated and enthused with your development plans and encouraged, not only to take an interest in them but also to get fully involved, this can have far-reaching benefits for the worldwide perception of your school. A well-communicated strategy for the future gives a sense of progress and purpose and it gets people talking. Your wider community is then proud to be associated with your success, and this will have spin-off benefits for the marketing of your school; for pupils applying to university and later on in the workplace. Moreover, everyone associated with your school – staff, pupils, parents and alumni – builds a team of enduring ambassadors, confident about your bright future and creating positive and far-reaching benefits for your school. Furthermore, as the word spreads and your constituents become engaged and enthused about the future, that commitment will translate into funds.

Important relationships

Most interested alumni, parents and friends of the school fall into one of three categories and in many cases more than one: they want to be involved; they are fond of the institution and in some cases they are high net worth individuals. *Forget the rest.* Even an alumnus who is 25 in the *Sunday Times Rich List* is a waste of time unless you can find some other way to connect with them, discover their passions and connect them to the future of the school.

The role of the development office is to build relationships with your community in order to identify the key groups who will take your development plan forward. They in turn will need their expectations managed. These groups include board members, volunteers, donors and major donor prospects.

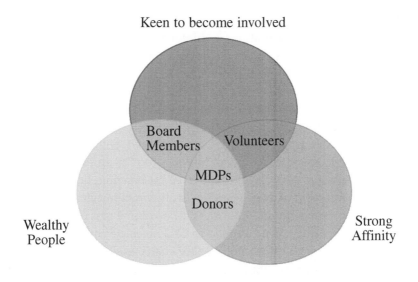

176

You then need to raise the awareness amongst all the relevant people in your school of where the overlaps in these categories are and what that means to the way they manage the same relationships.

There are few individuals in the United Kingdom and worldwide who do not give to some charitable or campaigning institution. They do this because they identify with the cause and because someone has asked them to support it. If we cannot justify the reasons why we need help, we cannot expect others to support us. When we have our development plan drawn up and have established the reasons for supporting it, we should feel confident about asking for money to achieve it.

Most schools have, or have had, a long-distance relationship with many of their alumni, and so we need to understand that building relationships takes time. During the process you will identify individuals who fall into all three categories and who become the major donor prospects (MDPs). These individuals could contribute the big donations that will make a real difference to your plans.

It's rather like asking someone to marry you: you wouldn't dream of doing it on a first date – and if you ask everyone you meet, you will soon get the wrong reputation. However, once you have identified the individual who is the focus of your attention, it is well worth taking time to build the relationship so that, when the time comes and you finally propose, you are confident that the answer will be 'yes'.

Remember too that in most cases a major donor has been a past donor and has given smaller amounts first.

Governors
You need to manage the expectation of governors first and foremost, as they are making a big investment in the development office. *It is vital that they too understand this process* – and that they are aware that the significant returns are unlikely to be in the short-term.

It takes approximately five years to recoup the investment and to see fundraising income start to grow. It is a key role of the development director to help the Head manage these expectations, by communicating strategy and future plans in a way that will engage not only the key

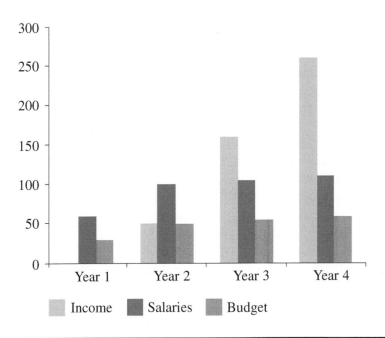

Income ▮ Salaries ▮ Budget

Benchmarks
Development Office costs will be 25% of funds raised
Average Total Costs £150,000
Average Salaries   £100,000
Average Budget   £50,000
Average no of Staff 2.9

stakeholders but also help them understand, and be patient about, the timescales involved. The diagram above illustrates this.

You need to study the history of appeals in your school. When was the last one? How much was raised and how long did it take? You are likely to find that 80% of the funds were raised from approximately 20% of the donors.

If, by simply sending an appeal letter to everyone, you raised reasonable or substantial sums, just think how much more could have been achieved if the major donor prospects had been identified, cultivated and engaged in the project *before* they were asked. Many schools have fallen foul of launching a fundraising campaign for a large capital project and then watching a totaliser creep skyward stubbornly slowly, as lots of cheques flood in for relatively small amounts. A percentage of your community may have given, but donors may also be bitterly disappointed at the slow progress.

Your governors also need to understand that a much better way of managing expectations is to make sure that you don't launch the appeal publicly until you already have pledges from your major donor prospects. This means that when, later on, the smaller gifts arrive, they will enable you to reach your target with apparent speed.

As a result, every donor can feel good that their contribution has made the difference. Many institutions boast of vast sums raised, but their strategy has nearly always been to secure a large proportion of the support *before* the launch to the wider public; to manage expectations and to make sure that everyone has the story straight before the launch.

Donors	1	2	3	5	10	20	50	100	Target
Gift Size £	500k	100k	50k	20k	10k	1k	100	50	
Total £	500k	200k	150k	100k	100k	20k	5k	5k	£1.08 M

Remember that, unlike a large national charity, your donor base is likely to consist of a few thousand people, not several million. This makes good groundwork a feasible proposition, even if your development operation is small-scale. So, if major donor solicitations are done quietly and you start to see pledges of support, you also have a much better idea of what you can expect to raise overall. By contrast, if everyone is turned off by the proposal during this initial 'quiet phase', it also gives the governors valuable time for a re-think.

Moreover, the governing body is a good place to test your case for asking people to give. If they have been instrumental in agreeing the strategy; if they are convinced it is a sound plan and that delivery is imperative, then they must be asked to support it financially themselves. If the governors, and even the senior staff, will not support the project themselves, there is a very weak case for asking anyone else to – so you must go back to the drawing board. It is not the amount that they commit that counts but rather the fact that they have contributed: their action represents a very powerful message sent out to the wider community.

Staff

Members of staff are other key stakeholders who, in the hectic environment of delivering lessons, marking work and meeting tight deadlines for tomorrow (or at best next week), often find it very difficult to think strategically. Take time to explain the process to them at staff meetings, and make sure that they too understand that fundraising is what happens when you do everything else right. Make sure they understand that if people *like* someone, they are likely to help that person – and that everyone in the school has a role to play in seeking that sense of collective approval!

Everyone is communicating something to someone about your school all the time; therefore we all have a duty of care to past students, parents and visitors. Any one of them could be a potential major donor. How we all look after them is very important. One misplaced word on the touchline or at a dinner party can undo months of hard cultivation work.

It is therefore vital to make staff aware of the development plan, the capital projects and the time it will take to raise the money. Some staff will also be in a position to give, and long serving members usually have a strong affinity with the school: cultivation of them too is time well spent. It is important to communicate successes in the strategy as you go along, so that all staff feel engaged and enthusiastic and help to maintain momentum.

Parents

Parents are facing the time of their lives when their commitments overall are at their most expensive. These often include huge mortgages and a multitude of other financial responsibilities.

In independent schools many of them are under the impression that school fees generate profit that can be used for capital projects. Thus the first step in managing their expectations is to make them aware that school fees or education authority funding often cover operational costs and maintenance, but do not provide significant sums for development.

Parents are always interested in major projects. However, they are less likely to be interested in the long term plans for your school, although they will be very keen on any developments that are likely to benefit their own children. In generating their interest it is very important that clear timelines are set, because without these their enthusiasm can quickly turn to disappointment.

Careful communication of development plans should incorporate short-term goals as well as the ultimate prize, so that everyone can see the progress that is being made. A report on giving, published every year, can be a valuable way of showing what has been achieved, and of generating that feeling of momentum.

The annual fund is a useful tool in managing parents' expectations, because short-term gains can be made by funding attractive projects that can be seen to be 'icing on the cake' for the benefit of all pupils – not least because they can generally be brought to fruition without much delay. The results will also help people to understand how much money can be raised from a broadly based appeal in one year, but that a more sophisticated approach is needed for a major capital project.

One of the pitfalls to be aware of with parents is that they sometimes want to use their support to influence outcomes that are particularly important to them and their own child or children at your school. For example, a focus on academic improvement leads to projects to boost facilities in the classroom, ICT provision, libraries, *etc.* However, the parent of a sporty child might think it is more important to acquire new liveried minibuses or even another AstroTurf pitch. This is the main reason why the development priorities that have been chosen need to be part of an overall strategy, communicated to everyone – and the focus must remain strong in order to achieve the goals.

To use my wedding analogy, it is rather like a wedding-present list: everyone wants to spend around £50 on the perfect personal gift, so the bride and groom end up with lots of tablecloths and toasters, whereas in reality the happy couple are saving for a 60-piece dinner service and are much more likely to complete it if everyone gives them a few plates. If donors want to support only their own pet projects, the effect of funds raised can be dissipated and it will take much longer to achieve the wider vision laid out in the development plan.

Pupils

Establishing the importance of a philanthropic culture is part of a child's education. As a consequence, an understanding of why schools are charities should be communicated to the pupils. It is worth making them aware of historical benefactions to their school, and the benefits that they enjoy thanks to the commitment of their predecessors.

Make sure that they understand the annual fund and the benefits they all derive from it: this will, in turn, give them a better understanding of why people must give back for the school to go forward. In time they will be approached to support their old school, so this is a golden opportunity to give them a lesson to carry through the rest of their lives: that whatever they can give will make a positive difference.

Alumni

This is by far the largest group of potential support in any institution, and it is well worth taking time to establish a good relationship with this constituency. Many former pupil societies think that schools are only after them for their money – and perhaps historically this has often been the case. They see the opening of a development office as a cover for fundraising, and a threat to their operation.

It is a priority for any development office to manage the expectations of this group – by explaining its role and building a relationship with the alumni that can be mutually beneficial. Administrative support for reunions; an up-to-date website; a good quality magazine that keeps them in touch, and a warm welcome whenever they can be persuaded to come back to school, should be the established norm before any fundraising is done.

Most people feel that their school days played a major part in influencing their lives, and as they grow older they are keen to meet fellow pupils, to see how those influences have manifested themselves in adult life. The development office should create as many opportunities as possible to facilitate that process and, where possible, to ensure that their *alma mater* is in the forefront of their thinking. In doing so, alumni continue to feel a strong affiliation to the institution and develop a life-long interest in sustaining its principles and securing its future.

Communicating the development plan to them is a different challenge, as they usually have very strong views on what is good and what is bad about your institution. Often their perceptions are out-of-date, but it is important to listen to their views and value their opinions. You can be sure that they will want the institution to develop and grow, and in listening to them you can tailor your communications to establish a strong case for support.

A regular feature in the alumni magazine on plans and progress will start to build interest in the future, as well as pride in the past. The school magazine should show the difference that donations have made to what has been achieved, and should take the opportunity to say 'thank you'. Frequent email contact that pulls alumni back to the website can ensure that they start to realise that they are still a valued part of the school family, and not simply a source of funds. Most of us will respond to a clear, exciting vision and will want to make a difference in the best way we can. Time taken in engaging your audience will reap significant rewards.

Critical success factors

At any stage in managing expectations it is important to respond to negative comments. Don't let them fester. Are there misunderstandings? If so, it is important to put them right. Are there perceived drawbacks to the scheme? You might need to re-think or re-work the proposal to minimise the objections by enhancing the positives. Agree in advance what the critical success factors in your strategy are and make sure they don't all relate to fundraising targets.

At the end of the first year the funds raised may well still be minimal, but as you enter the next phase, the following factors should be considered to measure success. The omission of one or more of these could have an adverse effect on the success of your development plans and future fundraising results.

- There must be a commitment from the trustees and governors to lead the fundraising process by example. Ownership must not rest solely with the development office.

- Your school must be perceived to be well governed, well managed and successful, not desperate for cash.
- Everyone associated with the school should be confident of its bright future.
- Finances should be sound and transparent to all.
- There should be evidence of support for the development plan from the whole school community.
- You should have clear identification of potential major contributors who will underpin the funding of your major projects.
- Respected, committed and influential individuals should be indentified who are prepared to lead the fundraising programme with the development director.
- Fundraising must not be geared towards debt reduction or routine maintenance.

If any of these are missing, you should not be afraid to acknowledge this, and to review the development plan and the case for support, then changing them for the better.

All these things should help you to manage your own expectations and will help you in your communication with key stakeholders to manage theirs, too. In this way you will drive your school's development forward.

Chapter 17

Formulating the
strategic plan

Tim Edge

First, to paraphrase Benjamin Franklin, 'by failing to plan you are planning to fail'!

It is important, however, that there is an essential balance between 'planning' and 'doing'. Plans should be succinct and target-driven but, once they are developed, the emphasis should be on cultivating members of your community; involving them in the work of your institution and, when the time is right, asking them to support you financially.

It is also important that plans are dynamic documents – constantly evolving around changing circumstances and priorities. As such it is therefore important that there is a mechanism for keeping plans under review and on track.

Success factors

There are a number of factors that will aid the formulation and delivery of the development strategy and the implementation of a successful fundraising programme:

- The full commitment of the Head and board of governors to the development programme.
- A perception that the governance and leadership of the school is effective.
- A clear and compelling vision of the way in which the school will develop over the next five to ten years.
- The perception that the school is run on a firm business footing with financial transparency.

185

- High levels of goodwill flowing to the school from its varied constituents.
- A significant number of respected and influential volunteers prepared to lead the fundraising programme.

If one or more of these factors is missing, plans need to outline how these challenges are being addressed.

It is essential that development plans dovetail neatly with those wider institutional plans formulated by the Head and board of governors. Imagine perhaps that a new Head and development director have arrived at the school at the same time, only to discover that there has previously been no proper strategic planning. How might they go about putting things in place?

Getting started

The first step is for the Head and governors to agree on the core purpose of the institution and its salient values. The core purpose (sometimes called the 'mission statement') should be succinct and aspirational, with the core values forming an accurate reflection of the essential characteristics of the organisation. Crucially, it should be easy to demonstrate that the core values are not just slogans, but can be vividly illustrated by what is happening on a day-to-day basis within the school. In short you have to be able to 'walk the talk'.

Development planning is a collaborative process, so the next stage is to survey all parents, teachers and pupils, to seek their views on how well the school is performing. This helps to identify not only the areas of strength, but also those that require more attention. This survey might be supplemented by workshops at which all sections of the school community are represented; these workshops reflect a brainstorming of the strengths of the school and the challenges confronting it.

From this collaborative process will spring strategic topics that will require greater analysis and examination. These might include:

- Recruitment and development of staff.
- Development of the curriculum.

186

- Raising academic standards.
- Personal development for all pupils.
- Enhancing the school's resources and infrastructure.
- Raising funds and building goodwill across the school community.

Once these strategic topics have been agreed, work can start in earnest on developing them. The bursary team, for example, will work up the section on resources and infrastructure. The pastoral team will work on the personal development of pupils and the academic team will examine academic standards and curriculum development. Of course, as part of this collaborative process, the development team will also be empowered to develop its own discrete plan, drawing on those strategic objectives handed down to them by the Head and governors.

Refining organisational objectives

In refining organisational objectives, it is important that development directors are allowed the freedom to produce their own departmental plans without too much prescription from above. One needs to avoid an over-emphasis on narrow fundraising performance, to the detriment of the need for proper relationship building. The following represent the kind of strategic objectives that might be handed down to a development director, and from which detailed development plans might evolve:

- To raise significant funds to meet the school's priorities.
- To create a true 'community of goodwill', where all members of the community are drawn closer to the school by news of its achievements and involvement in events and volunteering opportunities.
- To work in partnership with all departments, particularly the alumni relations department.

Measuring success

How do you measure success in this type of work? Setting fundraising targets will obviously depend on the needs of the school – for example, does it need to raise significant funds for major capital projects, or will the emphasis be on development of legacies, or on an annual fund? If the emphasis is on major capital projects, the development team will have to conduct some form of feasibility study into how much can be raised, and over what period of time.

In examining the feasibility of a fundraising campaign the following factors might be considered:

- What has been the past experience of the school in raising large amounts of money?
- How will the economic climate affect your fundraising aspirations?
- How have schools with similar profiles performed recently in the fundraising arena?
- How much goodwill is there in the wider school community?
- Is there a significant number of potential major donors in the school community?
- What is the quality of high profile volunteers who can help you execute your fundraising plans?

Setting fundraising objectives is one thing, but how might you measure the success of the development office in *non-fundraising* terms? This is not quite as challenging as it might seem. Demonstrating increased attendance at events over time is one good way of indicating increasing goodwill – as is an increased number of volunteers signing-up to help the school in a variety of activities.

Many schools are introducing web-based alumni management systems to help keep in touch with former pupils of all ages – particularly younger ones. The numbers of alumni regularly using your interactive systems and the growth of these numbers over time will give a strong indication of the levels of interest and engagement within your alumni community.

Of course it is very difficult to cultivate your alumni without the active commitment of the alumni relations office to this process. It is therefore important, particularly where the development and AR offices are not integrated, to include in the plan some headline objectives that emphasise the crucial importance of an active working partnership and how it might develop.

Preliminary research

Preliminary research matters a great deal. It is extremely important that the development office strategic plan is informed by the views of key members of the school community. The development director will already be aware of the Head's and governors' core objectives for development but these need to be supplemented by research.

These are just some of the key questions that should be addressed before the plan is drafted:

- What are the school's capital project priorities?
- How many of these should be supported by fundraising?
- How strong is the relationship between the development and alumni relations offices, and are there any obstacles to progress?
- How effective is the school's mechanism for communicating with its wider community?
- Does everyone understand what the school stands for, and the direction in which it is heading?

A succinct analysis of the strengths of the school and the challenges facing it can also be ideal preparation. Some might claim that SWOT analyses (strengths, weaknesses, opportunities and threats) are outmoded, but such a process is invariably helpful in teasing-out all the key issues facing the school and the development office. However, a SWOT analysis is always more effective when conducted as a group by, for example, the school's management team.

Key components of the strategic plan

Every plan should start with an index of pages and appendices. Make sure that the plan is split into functional chapters and that each page and paragraph is numbered for ease of reference.

The introduction to the plan might include a brief history of development activity at the school, to put the plan in context. Then the priorities of Head and governors for development should be outlined in a series of crisp bullet points. It is also important to touch on the SWOT analysis and the preliminary discussions that have taken place, as well as stressing the method for keeping the plan under review. It is often wise for the opening chapter of the strategy to be concerned with *cultivation*: the essential relationship building process which, if successful, will engender goodwill across your community.

Your preliminary discussions will have led you to an appraisal of the effectiveness of communications and cultivation activity across the school community, and the measures that need to be taken to improve it. Be careful to ensure that all sections of your community are considered in this section – particularly former parents, who often feel disenfranchised at the point their child leaves the school. It is often surprising how many former parents elect to stay connected with the school long after their child has left.

Whereas cultivation activity is aimed primarily at prospective donors, don't forget your existing donor community. Keep your donors in touch with the ongoing value of their gift to your organisation through a stewardship programme of events and communications.

The *fundraising* section of the plan should set out the priorities for fundraising and the methods for meeting these priorities. It is important to include a timetable for fundraising activity, so that the Head and governors are aware of what is to be achieved, and by which date. Always build enough preparation and research time into a fundraising timetable, and don't get rushed into starting major fundraising activity too soon. Err on the side of caution when forecasting: it is far better to under-promise and over-deliver than the other way round!

The main sub-headings of this section might include:

- Major gifts. How you intend to identify, engage and solicit potential major donors?
- Legacies.
- Stewardship. Your previous donors are your best 'customers'. Outline how you intend to keep former donors in touch with the value of their gift to your organisation.
- Annual giving. In this area, unlike when considering major gifts, it is the levels of participation, across your community, that are more important than the actual level of contribution. Annual funds are also

effective tools for identifying the major donors of the future.
• Support from corporate bodies and charitable foundations.
• Voluntary support and leadership.

If the development office is responsible for the school's *marketing*, this section should include observations on positioning; branding; PR profile; advertising; coordination of marketing; admissions and all the other varied components of the marketing 'mix'.

The section on *alumni relations* should review the current situation and the challenges influencing the effective provision of an alumni relations service. It is crucial in this section to emphasise the importance of the development and alumni relations offices working effectively together, as well as detailing the ways in which this synergy might be achieved.

The all-important section on *resources* should describe in detail the structures and the human and material resources necessary to deliver the development plans. Such detail might include:

• The role and composition of a major gifts group.
• The role of a separate steering group (monitoring progress against agreed targets).
• The location and equipping of the development office.
• The composition and roles of the development team.
• A three year draft budget (perhaps as a separate annex).
• Database proposals.

The strategy should end (or start) with an *executive summary* listing the salient recommendations, section by section.

Perhaps the most important section of the plan with regard to driving day-to-day activity is a *critical path timetable*. Normally on one sheet of paper, as a separate appendix, the critical path timetable lists, by functional area, what you plan to achieve, and in what timescale. It should also be quite clear from the critical path timetable precisely who is responsible for each specific task. Heads, governors and members of the development steering group find such critical path analysis to be a very useful tool in monitoring progress against realistic and agreed targets.

Meanwhile, in formulating and steering strategic development plans and evaluating their progress, it is always helpful to receive the support of key members of the school community. It is a good idea to put together a small steering group that can review the draft plans and make suggestions.

For example this group might comprise the Head, bursar and a key governor (often an alumnus/a). The governor should be carefully selected so that s/he can provide a bridge between the development office and the governing body, acting when necessary as an advocate for the development plans at board meetings.

Once the draft development office strategy plan has been signed-off by the steering group, the development director should be offered the opportunity to present the plans to the whole governing body in order to gain full corporate support. The steering group will also have an important role to play in ensuring that the plans are kept under regular review, and are adjusted in the light of experience.

Conclusion

Above all, despite the intricacies of the planning process and the complexity of the documentation, always keep the big picture in the back of your mind. Don't get lost in detail to the point at which you become paralysed by it. Focus instead on those major gift approaches, key events or communications initiatives that will make the biggest impact to the achievement of your overall goals.

And finally, once the plan is complete, the task now is to make it happen! As Frank W Woolworth once said: "Dreams never hurt anybody if you keep working right behind them to make as many of them become real as you can."

Chapter 18

Successful event management

Christopher Massi

Goodbye Saturday evening... School events occupy their own peculiar space in a school. One event has its origin lost in the mists of time; another is the passionate preserve of a parent group and the newest event is a black-tie dinner dance championed by a governor. As development director you will attend nearly every one of these, and at some point you will ask yourself whether you really signed up for all this, because the only thing that the events have in common is a near complete lack of common purpose – beyond disrupting your Saturday evenings.

You, of course, have your priorities for the school and you will soon express them not only through policy and practice, but also through the development office and perhaps through a fundraising campaign. But what do ferret races, the auction and old boys' day have to do with your priorities for the school? Probably not much at the moment, but with some planning and effective follow-up from your development office, they will.

If you have to give up Saturday night, make sure that the event still works for you on Monday morning. Every event should have value – value not necessarily measured in money raised that night, but measured in advancing your priorities longer-term.

In fact, the value of the event may be better measured not by whether it raised £15,000, but by whether it brought a new prospective donor to light, engaged an alumnus, or thanked an existing donor. The very eye-opening notion for most schools, the revolution in thinking, is that the event is not there primarily to raise money (seldom very much money) for the new arts building, but rather to serve the giving cycle.

In the giving cycle, the school works with prospective donors in five stages: identification, qualification, cultivation, solicitation and stewardship. Individual donors – the major donors who take part in the events as part of the school community – can often give much more in one cheque than the average school auction raises in an evening. But this does not necessarily mean the new Head needs to invent a new series of events, although the need for a new event might arise, depending on the type of school, its existing events, and campaign priorities. It is usually more economical and more politic to take advantage of existing opportunities.

Be thoughtful about your events and consider for a moment St Magritte's School. It has an excellent drama programme, but no theatre or rehearsal space. Most of the old boys (and old girls, who were first admitted to the school only recently) love the school, but they've gone on to become investment bankers and lawyers. A black-tie dinner-dance and auction on the 100th anniversary might raise £20,000, but that does not make much of a dent against the £3million cost of the new Head's proposed performing arts centre, which is to be his/her highest priority and signature mark on the school.

What role do the school's events play in finding £3million? Remember that you need to find potential donors; see whether they have the ability to give; engage them in your vision for the future; ask them for a gift; and then thank them.

Over at St Magritte's, they want to be nice to everyone, so they are going to make only slight adjustments to the existing events – and maybe add one or two opportunities for those prospective donors who can make a big impact. However, even then, there may be ways to involve the broader community.

The Head and director of development look at their event calendar, the giving cycle and the Head's priorities and come up with a plan, representing the five stages:

- Identification: St Magritte's needs to discover who is out there. The database of old boys was, until only recently, kept on file cards by the old boys' society (its members are only slowly waking up to the fact that theirs is now a coeducational school): they didn't want to surrender it to the school.

    Now that you've prised it away, you can start to identify prospective donors. The idea is to work out the best prospects in your possible universe of donors, and you do not want to invent too many new events or to spend time and money unnecessarily. So how does one find out who really cares about the school?

This is the stage where you cast a wide net to find your prospective donors. Here are three common events that might fit the bill:

a) Old boys' day. Hundreds of alumni turn up to play cricket, have lunch and take a tour. This year's tour at St Magritte's includes a walk through the crumbling theatre.

b) The music festival. A fine tradition at St Magritte's, when current parents and old boys stop by for a week of day and evening recitals. Sadly, the big recital had to occur in the crumbling theatre.

c) Opening night dinner for the play. Every year, the Head throws a reception before the opening night at St Magritte's for parents whose children are in the play and s/he invites along the governors and local alumni. Just a few nibbles and then up to the theatre which is, sadly, wholly inadequate for the expanding programme.

The key in every case lies in tracking who attends the event – and this is where most schools fall down. St Magritte's has fixed this problem and now the school tracks attendance in each former pupil's computer record.

After a few events, the school has noticed a trend: there is a core group of about 100 people showing up on a regular basis to school events: a mix of current parents and former pupils, plus a few governors who at a glance may have a few quid, but you aren't really sure.

• Qualification: development officers spend a great deal of time qualifying prospective donors: it really just means trying to work out who has the ability to make a significant gift and whether they have an interest in your school. Again, there is no need for St Magritte's to create a new event: the school is going to take advantage of two existing ones:

d) The drama support group quiz night. Every year this event raises £500 for drama and the parents are very proud of their effort. The Head of St Magritte's has glanced over the list of those scheduled to attend and discovered ten are already on his list of 100 former pupils and parents. He has managed to sit with five of them at dinner and discovered that they also serve on a committee at the Royal Opera.

e) The auction. This is often mistaken for a major fundraising event in itself (see below), but the real value of St Magritte's auction lies in seeing who bids for the week on the Riviera. Three bidders raise the price up to £10,000 and one of them is an old boy attending his third event at St Magritte's in a single year. The Head's eyes light up. His suspicions about the donor have been confirmed.

During the qualification stage, the Head and director of development worked out who had interest and ability, something they did not know before they began to use events more purposefully.

- Cultivation: this is all about engaging prospective donors in your mission and vision. Schools provide plentiful events at which this can happen, but they often fail to take advantage of them. The director of development and Head at St Magritte's have reviewed their existing school events and found several that they could easily adapt. They have then added some new events in London for those who cannot reach their leafy campus during the day:

    f) Every Friday, the St Magritte's sixth form invites a speaker to its assembly. With a quiet word, the Head has arranged for their next speaker, a hedge fund manager who loves West End theatre, to speak about funding for the arts. Just this once, they move the sixth form assembly to the school's crumbling theatre.

    g) Prospective donors, whether alumni or parents or friends of the school, need to become involved in the life of the institution. St Magritte's holds a careers night every year and with just a few adjustments, they have found a way to invite a few key donors to meet the school's best salesmen: its students.

    h) Some schools host alumni events for engineers so that old boys

196

can come together, trade war stories, do their networking and hear a few words from the Head. St Magritte's does that too, but it was time to put this event to work.

The Head has insisted that they cancel the upcoming networking event for elderly clerics and instead hold one for investment bankers at the office of a former pupil financier in the City. Now that their big prospective donor has been to a few events himself, he will say a few words before the Head speaks about how wonderful the school is – and how the Head just has to do something about that old theatre.

- Solicitation: from identification to cultivation and solicitation, it was a two-year journey at St Magritte's and the auction continued to tick along raising £20,000 each year. The Head enjoyed the evening and worked to ensure its success, but remembered that the auction was a tool for engagement and not a substitute for a proper face-to-face meeting with the donor about the school's priorities.

  Events (and this is really important) are not the best way to raise money. Events can help get you to the point where you ask for money, and they can be useful for thanking donors, but major gift discussions happen in private, unlike the venue for someone bidding for a cricket bat. See 'event traps' below.

- Stewardship: after the gifts came in and the Head was quick to send thank-you notes, s/he knew that s/he had to keep these great volunteers involved – and they wanted to stay involved because they were now huge supporters, financially and otherwise. The Head did invent a new event just for donors: a special invitation-only preview for the art show. The first year s/he hosted this event, it was in the art room. The second year, it was held in the foyer of the new arts centre. It was a big hit.

Event traps

Events are a tool to advance your mission (as above), but events also have a habit of taking on a life of their own. Below, you will find ways that they can go pear-shaped. Avoid these typical event traps and once again work to ensure they fit into the giving cycle. Here are a few of the more common traps, and for each, remember the solution: the event should either serve the mission of the school or be reshaped to do so. At the very least it should do no harm.

The auction. Financial reality and political reality exist in separate universes: no less true in the school than it is in Westminster. The financial reality is that auctions very rarely raise significant funds. Or to put it more accurately, they rarely *net* significant funds. Glance through the publicly available tax forms from schools in the United States to examine the evidence. Most schools seem to hold auctions; many break even; some make a little money; some show a loss, but very few make significant money. If these events were forced to show the amount of staff and volunteer time that went into them, virtually none would show a profit.

Take that same amount of time and effort and pour it into engaging major donors in mission-driven events: the sums raised will be much, much greater and the funds will go toward supporting your vision. A single major gift, which might take two or three years to materialise, could be five or ten times as large as the entire net proceeds of the auction. The financial realities of auctions are fairly clear: they are an inefficient way to raise funds for your cause.

The political realities, of course, are different. Auctions tend to have their own momentum, a larger constituency, and unfortunately goals that may or may not be consistent with your own. Donors who might otherwise give £100,000, give £5000 for the well-to-do rugby team to visit southern France, instead of giving to the bursary fund.

There are generally two options. Try to reshape the event so that it helps to identify and cultivate major gift prospects and supports school priorities, at least in part. Alternatively, step back and accept that you may not be able to change the event this year, but maybe you can lay the foundation for its evolution in the future. Take the long view.

We have always done this event. 'Always' in a school can indicate 'since last year' or 'since 1723', so it is important to consider whether the event is part of the institutional history or is something to which someone has become deeply, personally, irrationally attached.

Often enough, no single person claims an event and no one can remember why it happens in that way, on that day, and for what reason. It just reappears in the calendar every year because it was in the previous school calendar. Tempting as it may be to delete the event, you may wish to save the date, if not the actual event, since the space is already protected on your calendar and then renovate the occasion to suit your own purpose.

Parents' quiz night for our children's trip to someplace sunny. Five different sports with three different events per year: 15 opportunities to attend quiz nights, ferret racing, and dinner in the dining hall. It is a good opportunity to see parents and support the students, but 15 (or more) events may be pushing one's limits. These little events pop up like mushrooms. There is a danger in forcibly trimming them back: parents may take your pruning to mean that you don't support football/cricket/rugby/music. Consider instead shaping one or two of the events to suit your goals for the school. These often build school spirit, help to uncover potential supporters, and offer opportunities for you to advance your priorities.

Lock them all in a room. Surprisingly common, this event involves inviting parents, alumni and friends to an event where the purpose is to invite them into a room where they are given tea, biscuits and the impression that the door out has been locked. The Head then lectures the prisoners on why they should give. One might consider friendlier alternatives.

The governors' ball. From time to time, a governor will propose a black-tie benefit of some sort, the supposed purpose of which is to raise lots of money for the school. Without guessing as to the actual motive for a fancy dress party, please see item one (auctions) for advice on how to manage this idea.

We must have a Royal Visit. There may be a good reason to arrange such a thing: the 500th anniversary of the school's foundation, or perhaps a very close connection with the family. However, these visits are famously difficult to arrange and even more challenging to manage. The event may take a year of planning for a visit measured in minutes. (*NB* Planning a Royal Visit was described in *Senior Management Teams*, the second book in this series.)

Take a very close look at the cost/benefit of such a visit before going too far down this road, but if you do proceed, remember than any event, especially one that will take so much time and receive so much attention within your school community must, absolutely must, serve your mission and vision.

A few ideas

Schools are loaded with events: some right there and ready to go and some just waiting to be developed. If your school lacks the right event for your needs, consider one of these:

- Career networking: a great event for alumni to find new jobs and see old friends. Some schools arrange these by professional occupation with doctors, engineers, computer professionals, solicitors and so on.
- The leaving ceremony: schools with leaving ceremonies sometimes invite their alumni to participate. Participation can be as basic as being seated in the audience and then attending the reception, or as elaborate as processing to the stage in gowns for the 50 year leavers.
- The port and stilton rugby reception: while participation in sporting events tends to involve the young, old boys and girls of all ages can come to school for a reception at the rugby or cricket pavilion to watch current students play.
- The evening speaker: famous or interesting speakers often speak to parents and students at evening events. Consider inviting local alumni along, too.
- The art show opening: the event is already there, so think about the very few adjustments you might need to make to include prospective donors.
- The opening night: a buffet dinner before the opening night for the school play is a great way to involve potential parent and alumni donors, but one is, of course, always well-advised to have a sense of the play before going down this road!
- The scholars' dinner: stewardship events – and thank-you events – often receive the least notice, though they play a critical role in both thanking your supporters and ensuring that they feel well-inclined toward future giving. Consider having donors dine with your scholars one evening a year.

A final word on events

Events – lots of them – are going to happen. Rather than be swept along helplessly in their wake, remember that you can use them to advance your vision and to engage prospective donors in your plans for the school.

Anticipating the school events and keeping track of potential donors and the giving cycle seems a lot to manage with governors, students, applicants, teachers and staff knocking at your door, but you do have help. Keep your director of development close to hand. He or she is an expert at managing prospective donors and events. And don't forget to enjoy the event!

Chapter 19

Making the big ask

Neil Croucher

Asking someone for something is not always easy, particularly when you are asking them to give money – and even more so when it's a lot of money. Not everyone can do it, and there are many pitfalls along the way. The process can take a long time, and it can sometimes be tedious and time consuming, but the benefits for the organisation can ultimately be huge and rewarding. Moreover there is no getting away from the fact that making the 'big ask' is central to what a good development director's job involves.

However, long before the 'ask' itself, you have to know what you are asking for. Your request should be part of a long-term development programme that is both sustainable and deliverable, in order that the donor can see an integrated plan of development for the school or college, stretching well into the future. This may sound distinctly basic, but you would be surprised at the number of organisations that just ask for the one big gift, without putting it into context or presenting their request in a professional, businesslike manner.

We all dream of discovering the ideal or 'dream' donor. An archetype might be someone whose giving potential has been unknown to anyone else (thus affording us the intense satisfaction of having made the important discovery); someone who loves our particular institution purely for what it already is; who can be convinced with a minimum of time and effort that our school is the one organisation to which s/he has always wanted to lend support; who comes with no hidden agenda and who will impose no conditions on the gift; who has no dependent relatives to inherit their money; who offers us the distinct possibility of further gifts to come.

The reality tends, of course, to be somewhat different. Thanks to the growth in development prospect research, potential donors tend to be known to a number of organisations all playing on their emotions, loyalties and aspirations and all seeking to convince such people of their unique worthiness. The donors themselves are likely to have attended several schools and universities in their time, all of which now have them in their sights; they may well have many other potential calls on their generosity, which are completely unconnected with education (remember the anecdote at the start of chapter 12). It's just possible that they won the lottery, or inherited a fortune from some distant member of the family, but it's more likely (say) that they have built up a business, and then perhaps sold it. If this is indeed the case, they won't have made that business the success that it is by having been a soft touch for every passing good cause.

Above all, they are likely to be skilled and experienced at differentiating between causes and projects that are genuine or bogus; business plans that are well constructed or poorly thought out. Always expect them to come with firm views, willing to be convinced, but only on their terms. Never expect them to be a push-over.

So how do you go about it all? The ongoing school development plan can, and should, provide the organisation with a root and branch review of existing facilities, along with the planned programme for new building and a wish list for the next five or so years. Donors are interested in investing in a planned programme rather than a 'one-off knee jerk' reaction to fundraising. Most gifts, once made, will be followed up by continuing interest in the organisation and a keenness to support their investment in it in a wider sense. Then, after a period of time, we hope there will be further financial help with the rest of the plan.

Seamless and confident planning is not always as easy as it sounds. With change comes nervousness within the staff and governing bodies. It is vital that they too own the development plan and are part of its implementation and delivery. The plan should be reviewed every year; its progress noted and reported; donors and staff informed. It should then be updated as one year's projects are achieved and drop off the list, while other, newer ones take their place and start to move up from the bottom.

Assuming that the plan is now in place, we need to identify the major donors:

- Who are they?
- What relationship do we have with them?
- What is their wealth?
- How do we get close to them?

In a boarding school it is often the housemasters and housemistresses (HMs) who have the closest contact with the parent body, whereas it is the alumni association that has closest contact with the former pupil body. I have found informal meetings with those groups to be the most fruitful route in helping to identify our potential major donors.

The parents have a vested interest in seeing the school at the forefront of independent education. The alumni, especially when they get older and have achieved much in their own lives, look back on their schooldays with pride and thankfulness. This attitude is not always the case when they are younger; making their way in the world; having children of their own and carrying big mortgages – and their enthusiasm tends to grow with the passing of the years.

HMs and the alumni association have very different roles to that of the foundation or development office. The HMs collectively have care of the children (working with their parents), and the alumni association has a role in keeping the old boys and girls together. If fundraising was rammed down everyone's throat at every meeting, they would soon walk away from it all. However, the development office can, and must, have a role that is very close to both organisations. The key influence-formers must all be aware of the development plan, and how it will be integrated into the life of the school.

Having seen all the appropriate bodies (which includes the school admissions department) and having collected a list of potential major donors, the serious research can begin. This is a vitally important part of the process. We do not want to go to someone asking for something that is well beyond their means, and therefore embarrassing them. On the other hand we do not want to be asking for a small sum when the potential donor is quite capable of giving a lot more.

That can be equally embarrassing: it suggests that we cannot be bothered to research our prospects properly, and that we underestimate their previous career success. Our prospects expect our time and respect in such ways. We also need to assess whether we should be asking for a lump sum, gift aided up, or maybe down by taking the gift aid off the total sum, thus making the gift appear smaller to the donor than its 'real' value will be to us.

The research can be done through information that is in the public domain and often available via the internet. A Google search is a good way to start, and a prospect's home address usually gives some indication as to his or her wealth. Companies House will have information on the number of boards on which the prospect sits, or other associations with which he/she is connected.

For instance, if the donor is on the board of a large art gallery or similar prominent institution, that will usually mean s/he has donated to it and also has a passion towards that particular area. All this information will enable you to fit them appropriately to the 'ask' you are about to make. Companies House annual reports also give information about shareholders or individuals in that organisation at board level, and many companies reward senior people partly in shares.

So, now you have built up a broad profile of the individual, and you know something of what they are interested in and what might motivate them to give. As the next step, the research and the development plan need to come together.

You will now have to decide who is going to get to know this person. In this role the development office may be merely the facilitator, actively involved only with the friend-raising process. To start the process, I ask for an invitation from the HMs to gatherings based in the boarding houses, or to year-group meetings. We have sometimes used dinners with small groups of people to host an occasion where the friend-raising process can be developed. I also use the sports fields for this purpose – but not for overtly chasing individuals.

However it is done, the aim is to get to know the individual(s) a little better. It is important at this stage to include the person who is going to do the 'ask'. This will usually be the Head, or chairman of governors/foundation. But the 'ask' must always be made at a senior or peer group level.

You are now armed with the research: you know something of the background of your prospect; what good causes s/he has given to in the past; what his or her shareholding might be in certain companies, and approximately what s/he earns. All you have to do is make the 'ask'.

The development office should give the 'asker' a full and detailed briefing before the event. I always like to go along when the 'ask' is made, although I also recognise that on some occasions my presence may turn out to be inappropriate, and that I shall then need to think on my feet and improvise my plans accordingly.

How to make the 'ask' is a very individual process. A potential donor should already know about the existence of the development programme, and we now need to put him or her in the privileged position of making it, or one of its component projects, come to fruition. If, for instance, you have identified a new performing arts centre as your key project for this meeting, tell the potential donor about the benefits that such a building would have to the life of the organisation, and why it is so desperately needed. Then say what it will cost, and be specific about the amount you require from him/her as a donor.

Then comes the difficult bit! Stop talking and let him/her talk – if they wish. This part of the process is not for the faint-hearted: it involves a degree of nerve. The way *not* to proceed is to see a silence as deeply embarrassing, and then quickly to get the conversation moving again by downgrading the amount you have just asked for.

By doing that, you could end up with £5000 instead of £500,000. The fact is that your prospect is probably just thinking of how s/he can actually give you the amount you want. Should it be over a period of time? Or is it tax deductible? Can I make my gift from my personal wealth, or can my company contribute? What will my wife/husband think about it? All these thoughts will be racing round inside your prospect's head.

There are plenty of other issues that can be discussed to dispel any period of silence. These include incentives that attract certain donors, such as naming opportunities – either for a whole building, or a classroom or some other space. There is also the question of whether the whole gift is made at once, or over two or five years, and then the very important issues of tax. If your donor has a large shareholding, a gift can be made towards the project in a very beneficial way: this is in itself a strong argument for the presence of the development director at such encounters, to explain the technical intricacies of tax efficient donations. However, in my experience, the donor will generally prefer to discuss the tax situation with accountants if s/he is considering a major gift.

Give people time to think, rather than just saying: "We want your gift here and now." Explore all the possibilities; make it clear that you understand that they may need time to talk to their families; discuss whether it will be a public or private donation, or if they will accept a naming opportunity. That is all good material for when you meet them for the next discussion.

My favourite 'ask' was with a certain Master of Marlborough, in a forest in a foreign country (I shan't tell you where). We knew that our host liked a cigarette; at an opportune moment I asked him to come and sit by the fire to have one, and the three of us withdrew from the family table. At that point the Master outlined the development programme; the particular building for which we wanted funding, and the amount required.

There was a difficult silence, of the type already described. Our prospect then said he would make the payment that we had requested in two lump sums: one payable at the beginning of the year, and one at the end. He kept to his word, and the amount given was over £1 million. He has since gone on to do even better things for us as our relationship has developed.

Every organisation like ours has these kinds of people. But they are not to be messed with, and the whole process should be treated with care and respect. Many other staff neither see nor understand this patient, painstaking process going on in a development office, and they judge the development team's success only by the published results to date. Yet this 'tracking' process can sometimes take years to happen, and the rewards for the institution can be very great in the end. In the same way as with legacy giving, the major gifts opportunities have to be nurtured and carefully handled.

Finally, the part that so many people (even the more successful fundraisers) are surprisingly poor at: saying "thank you". Naturally, at the end of our meeting we say "thank you", and in its immediate aftermath we write effusive letters, but so often we then allow these major donors to cool off and drop away. The one thing you can be reasonably sure about is that this person is now committed to your school: it is likely, in time, that s/he will donate again.

Saying "thank you" requires the development office to be in regular, but not intrusive, contact with donors; inviting them to special occasions (for instance, when the governing body meets, or an opening ceremony takes place) and to a special celebration dinner afterwards. Invite them to concerts or Christmas plays or carol concerts: just make them feel special. Never underestimate the power of birthday and Christmas cards: they are only small things but they do mean a lot. They show that we are thinking of our supporters and that we do not take them for granted.

The other very important thing about this whole process is the documentation of the database. Every letter and phone call should be noted, along with the outcomes and results. The information held there must be extremely confidential to the development office and the Head. We happen to use the Raisers Edge package, which seems to perform these functions adequately and without too much difficulty, but there are also other brands on the market.

None of these processes are difficult, but in some cases they can be time consuming. At other times, however, success can come very quickly. Another major donor came for lunch and wrote the cheque out on his first visit. The whole process took 1 hour and 20 minutes. However, as the experienced professional will know – that does not happen very often! So:

- A coherent and deliverable development plan.
- Establish your major donor potentials.
- Research.
- Friend-raise.
- Ask.
- Thank.
- Keep in contact.

Happy hunting!

Chapter 20

Fundraising tactics

The annual fund

Elisabeth Anderson

The annual fund is the backbone of every development office and will generally inspire the first gift that a donor will make to your institution. No matter how large or small, old or young, with or without wealth your constituent base is, your school needs an annual fund.

The annual fund reaches out to every single one of your constituents: former pupils, parents and supporters – and it asks them to contribute to your school's needs. The widest participation is what is of prime importance for such a fund, not necessarily the size of gift. It seeks their support each and every year, and it is for projects for the here and now. It is building a better today, where everyone can make a difference.

Annual fund check list

- Identify need.
- Case for support.
- Seeking funds.
- Donor cycle.
- Make giving easy.
- Reporting.
- Stewardship.

Identify need
The annual fund supports small-scale projects that are not included in the school's budget, but are essential to the quality of the education you

provide. In most cases you will ask for:

- Money that you can direct to wherever the school needs it: *ie* mostly unrestricted funds for the school to direct, as needs arise throughout the year.
- Bursaries: *ie* your school's financial assistance programme for students.
- Contributions towards small-scale projects such as equipment or facility upgrades, but not for repair and maintenance projects.

The bursar will have the most comprehensive list of departmental needs and priorities, so it is important to start with him or her. Equally though, presenting the concept of the annual fund to all the heads of departments is a great way to involve the common room in the development operation, and to gain their 'buy in'.

Ideally, you are looking for projects that will have a major impact on a wide range of student life and interests, such as academics, sports, arts, music and science activities. Once you have your short list, it is vital to engage with each department; to find out why their project is important *now*, and the benefits you expect it to provide.

The case for support
Your case for support is not a list of what you need, but a compelling story of how students' lives are improved and their experiences transformed. Inspire your constituents about your school today: cite recent successes, academic excellence and sporting achievements. Create a feeling of overall success, but emphasise that school fees alone cannot support all the projects needed to provide educational excellence. With modest annual support from all constituents, your school will maintain the level of quality that parents and former pupils have come to expect.

Seeking funds
There are three primary methods for seeking annual fund donations:

- Direct mail.
- Telephone campaigns.
- Face-to-face meetings.

Direct mail

Direct mail is the most efficient and least intrusive method of reaching the highest number of your constituents. You will include everyone on your list, except those identified as major donors or major prospects, who will be invited to a face-to-face meeting.

Using your case for support, you will write a letter and design a brochure to outline the particular projects you are seeking to fund. When designing your annual fund mailing, you will want to consider:

- Personalised 'ask' amounts, based on previous gifts, location and age, as appropriate.
- Asking for regular commitments, not just single gifts.
- Personalised letters and reply forms, and personally signing as many as possible – within reason!
- Colour images: they are an effective way of enhancing your case, although they can add to the cost.

Although direct mail reaches the largest number of constituents, understandably it has the lowest return. It is hard to predict what an acceptable return may be, although it is typically between 2% and 10%.

Web-based social networking has transformed the way in which we connect with our former pupils for events and reunions, so it will also change the way in which we raise annual funds by direct mail, especially with younger generations.

Telephone campaigns

Telephone campaigns are the best way to engage with the highest number of your constituents in the most personal way.

Generally, campaigns are held annually or biennially during a two or three week period, when you will hire a team of recent leavers from your school. The callers will be trained in calling techniques, and how to ask for and secure a gift. Recent leavers are excellent ambassadors for your school and your former pupils will enjoy hearing about how the school has changed since their day.

To select your call list, you will identify a group from within your entire constituency based on availability of telephone numbers, age range and giving history. You will need approximately three prospects for every completed conversation, and you can expect to receive a 50% giving rate from those conversations, with half of the gifts being paid by direct debit.

Telephone campaigns give you the flexibility to segment donor groups and to focus your efforts. You may wish to focus on non-donors, or on those whose current pledges are ending, or on donors who may not have given for a number of years. The callers have enough information to help direct the conversation, in order to achieve the best results, matching the case for support with personal interests.

Although telephone campaigns are largely a fundraising exercise, affinity calls (particularly to younger constituents) allow you to build long-term positive relationships. However, phone calls can be viewed by some people as intrusive: therefore you will always send a pre-call letter to all those you intend to call, with an opt-out option.

Telephone campaigns require significant administrative support, which includes signing and sending letters; reviewing data; entering results; tracking feedback and following up pledges. Do not underestimate the valuable information that you will acquire, and make sure it is correctly tracked for future campaigns and meetings. Many schools engage consultants to help with telephone campaigns.

Face-to-face meetings

Face-to-face meetings are used to cultivate high net worth individuals, whom you believe to have the inclination to make significant donations to your school. Major donors account for 10% of your donors, and yet they will give 90% of your overall budget. They will be among the first people you approach in a capital campaign.

It is important to remember that over 80% of donors who make significant donations began with gifts of less than £250. Thus the annual fund is an excellent way to meet with major prospects, and to build relationships and trust, before approaching them for a significant gift.

Due to the time commitment, face-to-face meetings will be pursued with only a limited number of major donors and major prospects, but you can expect a 75% gift return from these meetings.

Donor cycle

Step 1 – New donors

The first step in the donor cycle is to convert a non-donor into a donor. Once they become a donor, no matter how much the gift is worth, you will begin to engage with them in a more personal way.

Step 2 – Renewing support

Once a donor has made their first gift, you will approach them asking for their renewed support. At this stage, you are concerned with a repeat gift, ideally of an equal amount.

Step 3 – Increasing gift amounts

As the relationship develops, you will better understand what motivates the donor to give. You can now discuss with them how they might increase their gift amount and identify areas of interest that will result in a larger gift.

Make giving easy

Make it as easy as possible for donors to give you money!

- Accept cheques, credit cards, electronic transfers and direct debits.
- Set up online giving with a link on your website.
- Increase gift amounts using Gift Aid, for UK taxpayers only.
- Learn about tax efficiency with legacy giving, stock transfers and higher rate taxpayers.
- Establish a foreign charity, if appropriate, to give tax benefits in other countries.
- Learn about Transnational Giving Europe (TGE) to give your European donors a way to make tax efficient donations.
- Communicate all methods of giving on gift forms and on your website.

Reporting back

From a donor's perspective, they want to know that their money will benefit the students whom they seek to support, and that their gift is being used wisely. Building trust with annual fund donors is imperative, as their loyal support pays great dividends in the future. Therefore, you must report back to them, letting them know how their gift has made a difference.

At the end of each year, you will produce a report on giving, which lists all donors (but always give donors the option to remain anonymous), and outlines your campaign and funding successes. Send it to all of your constituents, not just to donors, and always enclose a gift form and return envelope.

Stewardship

Thank you, thank you, thank you – there are never too many ways to thank your donors!

Begin with a phone call from the development director for each and every gift; send a thank-you letter signed by the Head; invite all donors to an annual donor reception; invite the top 50 donors each year to lunch; include 'thank you' calls in your telephone campaigns; send updates on specific projects of interest; invite them to school concerts and events, and more.

Summary

Set realistic goals, particularly when launching an annual fund. Donors will be more likely to repeat their donations if they see that you asked for what you need, and spent it on what you asked for. As the trust builds, so will the annual fund. Reporting back on funding successes is the golden rule for the annual fund.

The best month to begin your annual fund campaign is in October. Why? Because it is near the beginning of the academic year, and it is the one month when we are not distracted by Christmas, taxes and holidays!

To run a successful annual fund campaign, you will need to invest in resources. These include people; technology; administration and more. If you do not have in-house expertise available, the use of consultants can save you time and money.

Overall, for every £1 spent, you can expect to receive £4 in return from donations. Simply put, the annual fund strengthens the 'culture of giving' within your whole community, and is for all schools and all constituents.

Legacy campaigns for former pupils

Richard Owen

As the development director in my present post for 13 years, legacy fundraising has been a very important part of my work. During this time we have successfully raised over £1 million in legacy income from some 100 former pupils. More recently we have been left around ten legacies a year, varying in amount from £100 to over £750,000.

In addition we have over 250 people – former pupils and staff and current parents – who have informed us that they have pledged a legacy in their will. In reality, not all of these people will have actually done this and people often change their minds. However, on the other side of the coin, many legatees never disclose their will to anyone apart from their solicitors, and therefore there is every reason to assume that other legacies have been left to us of which we currently have no knowledge.

The majority of the legacies that we have received to date are from former pupils who are married and have dependents, but these have been for £1000 or less. We have twice received legacies of over £500,000 but in both cases the legatee was single, with no dependents. As with all forms of fundraising, it is important to focus on your best prospects. These seem to be former pupils and staff, again with no dependent relatives.

Whilst all schools are different, I would expect that much of what I have experienced holds true for most UK schools.

The legacy market in the UK

Nationally, legacies currently provide charities with over £1.9billion each year and they are the largest source of income from individuals. The average legacy value to a charity is £19,000. 87% of people die leaving some form of will. A minimum of four years typically elapses between the last update of a person's will and their death, but more realistically some 30 years or more might elapse between the time that a will is made and the funds being ultimately received. Encouraging legacy donations is, therefore, a very long-term fundraising process, and runs in tandem with

215

other fundraising strategies to persuade a potential benefactor to support a cause – either with gifts of time or money.

Aim: to build a long-term relation and foster goodwill with potential donors

In order to 'cherish' and sustain a long-term dialogue with potential legatees, we aim to find appropriate ways to keep in contact. This can be done in a low-key, unobtrusive manner; for example, by inviting them to venues that might be of interest to them, or reunions with fellow staff or pupils.

When the time is right to discuss legacies, potential donors should never be asked for a specific indication of how much they will leave: this is intrusive and can be counterproductive. The key is gently to persuade people to pledge a legacy, and then continue with supportive contact to ensure that they keep your school in their will until they die.

Communications

Our main means of communications takes the form of regular adverts and articles in school and former pupil publications. In these we give examples of past legatees and demonstrate the difference that their legacies made, and still make, to the school – and to current and future pupils. The 'drip-drip' of this type of information can make a significant impression on legatees.

We also believe in tactful references and comments made in speeches; for instance legacy storytelling, given by the Head at specific former pupil reunions. It is important to have a basic legacy leaflet to hand out at reunion events, or for loose inserting in other relevant publications. However, more detailed information sheets on the various types of legacies, codicil forms and appropriate wording for wills, should also be available on request and on the school website.

Every four years or so, we write to a specific cohort (for example former pupils over the age of 50) to ask them to consider leaving a legacy to the school. The letter should be written by someone who knows, or who has something in common with, the other recipients. For example they might have been a former secretary of the alumni association and therefore well known to a large number of former members of the school. Or they might be of a similar age. The following letter is an example of this strategy and was recently sent to all alumni over the age of 50. It resulted in us receiving over 100 positive replies.

But for...

It wasn't a happy day when, at the age of ten, I was summoned to my prep school Headmaster's study to be told that my father had died. He was just 40, leaving a young widow, four children and not much cash. I had enough to think about in the following weeks without worrying about my planned future at the school – a school about which my father was passionate.

Then came news that an anonymous benefactor had offered to pay my school fees right through to my leaving. I still don't know who that person was but I can think of few greater gifts to a young man in my situation. Without those days at the school I simply cannot imagine how my life would have worked out.

That's why I have made provision in my will to help fund bursaries at the school for those kids who would otherwise, through lack of funds, be cheated of the education I enjoyed.

It's as simple as that.

I hope you, too, may be inspired by my benefaction to do the same. Yours *etc.*

Legacy society

We established a legacy society ten years ago as an invaluable way of focusing attention on the importance of legacies, and at the same time providing us with a way of thanking legacy donors while they are still alive. The society currently has 250 members. We arrange an annual event at a prestigious location in London every year, which is extremely popular!

Legacy committee

In all forms of fundraising, the use of active volunteers is vital. We have a legacy committee that consists of half-a-dozen former pupils and staff, all of whom are volunteers and are themselves legacy donors. They offer invaluable advice and expertise. We meet regularly to discuss our legacy strategy and potential legatees.

Finally

Decide who your major legacy prospects are. As will be clear by now, major legacy donations tend to be received (in my experience, at least) from former pupils and staff without dependents. It is this sector of our former pupil body, and staff, whom we are keen to identify and to invite back to functions at the school, in the knowledge that they should have the greatest ability to make the largest legacy gifts, if they choose to do so. Remember, too, that legacy fundraising can have huge benefits in the long term. If you start your campaign now, do not expect significant results for at least four years. So the sooner you start, the better!

Over the years, I have come to rely on the knowledge and expertise of legacy consultant Richard Radcliffe. He is an acknowledged expert in this field and I am very grateful for his advice and input to this article.

Conclusion and overview

Nick Pettingale

Without a doubt, the role of the development professional is now integral to the future of independent schools in the UK. But then I would say that wouldn't I? As a development professional I have a vested interest, and as chairman of the Institute of Development Professionals in Education (IDPE), I have a responsibility to state it.

However, I do not believe that you can read this book without becoming increasingly aware of the growing financial pressures on our current and future parent body. It will no doubt need greater bursarial support in coming years. I also believe that you cannot have even a nodding acquaintance with the state of the national finances and think otherwise.

Our schools need, more than ever, a professionally overseen development strategy; assistance in implementing the best of good business practice and someone to stand alongside the Head and keep an eye on the future, whilst we do what we are called to do. That is educate children.

You will have read much in this book that has been practical, down to earth, clear, simple advice, good processes and techniques but what about...

Emotions and attitudes

Our schools are uniquely positioned to generate and become what Kevin Roberts, CEO Saatchi and Saatchi Worldwide, calls a 'love mark' (as opposed to a trade mark). Our schools generate huge feelings of warmth, love and loyalty from our past students, and sometimes even from current parents, which is beyond reason and logic at times. However, so much of this love and warmth can lie dormant and untapped without a professional development strategy in place. Someone to take responsibility to capture, coordinate and channel that goodwill; to benefit the school of today and our students of tomorrow.

'Fostering in all those who care, a lifelong interest in sustaining its principles and securing its future', as Jane Vines put it so well. People buy with their emotions and then justify the purchase with reasons and facts, not the other way round. This is true of education and true of our donors. Way back in the history of your school an individual, or a small group of people, came together to provide education driven by, first, seeing a need and then, secondly, by their own values and beliefs. Those values and beliefs drove not only what they wanted to achieve but also, and more importantly, *why* they wanted to achieve those goals.

It is the *why* that must be understood and captured; taken with us and made relevant in today's society. For example 'social inclusion' and bursarial support isn't simply a trendy bandwagon that others are seeking to ride, driven by changing charity laws. It is, one hopes, integral to the culture and ethos of the school.

However, the way we now deliver social inclusion might need to change. So might boarding within a more mobile society; sports; the concept of leadership and discipline; and our school's connection with the local community. But in all of this we must not lose sight of our reason to be in development or to have a development operation: we are about education; our 'end products', to put it crudely, are some of the most outstanding young men and women in the country. That is why we do what we do.

Schools have often traded on their history; survived on legacies and bequests that arrived largely through luck; experienced big one-off appeals that many times failed and sometimes left a bad taste with donors. Then a fanfare in the common room heralds the arrival of the new development director and a new era of fundraising begins with 'now you're here, people will start giving us money?' Or, as I was once introduced to a current parent: "This is Nick, the school's 'conman'."

My passion for education was shaped during the 1985 famine in Ethiopia. My three sponsored children, Sahi, Elsa and Meme, all had their lives and the future of their families altered forever by the power of education. Development is not simply about 'bringing in a few quid' or even a few million quid, to build that new science block, for instance. It is about children, students, education and relationships that are formed by them that last a lifetime.

If, as a development professional, you had lost sight of that, I hope this book has rekindled your fire for the children in your care; and if your Head,

220

bursar or governors have lost sight of that message, I suggest you give them this book, gift wrapped for Christmas. Oh, and include a Gift Aid form.

A healthy attitude to running a development department is to manage it as though it were your own business. When, in a previous life, I was a self-employed graphic designer, I knew that most business was about networking and the long-term relationships one sustained. Repeat business is the life blood of a profitable company. Having won a contract I also had to invest time in the ensuing relationship, or I would be starting all over again in a few months' time. I lived with an urgency and a sharpness (generated because my mortgage was on the line each month) that is so often missing within the security of large and historic institutions.

Information
Another important aspect of our work, often overlooked, is information; it is the life blood of a development office. Using a questionnaire, which gathers information covering personal contact details: time at school; hobbies and interests; directorships and current employment is crucial. The information and research that can be uploaded on to the database and easily retrieved is vital.

There is no virtue in having thousands of names and masses of information on a database that simply sits there year on year and does not reflect meaningful connections with your school. We need our Heads to position us properly within the school's organisational structure in a position that enables us to see and influence where the school is heading and that gives us credibility in the common room.

Technology
An interactive website, social networking sites and message texting are all new technologies that can act as a conduit for all alumni by keeping them connected to the school and each other, and attracting back those who have lost that connection over time. There is no doubt that we live in days where technology is advancing at a rapid rate: when Sir Timothy Berners-Lee invented the World Wide Web in 1989 there were only a 1000 internet devices that could access it. Today there are more than 1,000,000,000. The first commercial text was sent in December 1994;

today more texts are sent everyday than there are people on the planet.

No longer are donors, certainly not major ones, simply writing cheques because you ask them to. Rather they are following their money with their influence and skills. A good development director will be building bridges that harness those skills, way before a gift is ever sought.

And finally...

If you are still not convinced, ask yourself the following: do you have all of the professional development funds you need to provide for now and the future? Do you have all the facilities in place for now and the future? Do you have 'state-of-the-art' IT facilities and all the buildings you need to deliver a first class education in a rapidly changing world?

If the answer to any of these questions is 'no', then ask yourself where are you going to get them from, because tuition fees alone cannot keep up with the need for change, expansion and improvement. The answer is: you need to a have a professionally-run development office that can create new income streams and help you to market the school and to recruit students.

Your development director needs a clear vision and a strategic plan; good information and research; supportive and involved colleagues; a focused, fun events programme; a healthy relationship with the alumni association; and the time and space to lay good, solid foundations that will pay dividends in the future. Not much to ask, is it? However, with those things in place, together we can, and will, be making a huge difference, not just now but for another couple of centuries.

"You can't change the world," said Mother Teresa, "but you can change somebody's world." That's what we do.

What AMDIS and IDPE can offer you

AMDIS

The Association of Marketing and Development in Independent Schools, founded in 1993, has been promoting best practice in the independent education sector for over 15 years. We represent schools rather than individuals, have over 400 member schools and are growing every day!

We run workshops, conferences, seminars and networking lunches. Our newsletter, online news and everything on our website is available to anyone within a member school. For full details, see: www.amdis.co.uk

Those with a part or full-time responsibility for marketing and development find that AMDIS not only develops their professional knowledge but is also invaluable as a network – there is such a wide range of experience within AMDIS that there is always someone to learn from or to help.

Find out more about the benefits of becoming a member by contacting us or coming along along to one of our events.

AMDIS, 2 St Michael's Street, Malton, North Yorkshire YO17 7LJ
Tel: 01653 699 800
Email: enquiries@amdis.co.uk

IDPE

The Institute of Development Professionals in Education's regional networks are one of the most valued aspects of our work. There you will meet, generally twice per year, with fellow professionals and receive advice, support and shared ideas that will strengthen you and your work in your school.

We are set to launch the Essential Development Tool Kit, a modular training package that is geared to those new to development or with less than two years' experience. In addition our spring seminars are focused on experienced practitioners who are served by a network of internal and

223

external experts who take a more in-depth look at subjects.

Our annual conference is more popular than ever and we have a growing network of the industry's best consultants and service providers – all of this to serve you, the development professional and through you, to serve your Head and your school.

For further information about membership, and to find your nearest regional co-ordinator, please contact:

Jo Woods, IDPE Business Manager
Tel: 0845 299 8851
Email: info@idpe.org.uk
Website: www.idpe.org.uk
Registered office: Suite 33, 10 Barley Mow Passage, London W4 4PH

Afterword

An extract from *Pretty Baby*, by Alan Coren

On 31st January, 1976, The Times launched a humorous short story competition with a 3000 word piece by Alan Coren, who died in 2008 and who was surely one of our finest satirical writers. We are very grateful to Times Newspapers Ltd for permission to reproduce these extracts.

Coren described the arrival into this world of little Wotan, the perfectly-formed first-born child of Nigel and Felicity Couchgrass. Nigel was creative director of an advertising agency; Felicity, a tireless supporter of radical causes, never long out of the news spotlight. With genes like that, adored and spoiled by parents who were determined to take every commercial advantage of his perfect form by launching him into the advertising world through Nigel's media company, little Wotan's future seemed assured…

'It is said that when little Wotan Couchgrass sprang from his mother's womb, his first action was to bow towards the arc-lights; his second action, it is as frequently said, was to spin in the obstetrician's lubricated hands and attempt to gum through his own umbilical cord.

It is said, of course, now. At the time, commentary upon the birth and its star was confined to astonished murmuring at little Wotan's immaculate beauty. Birth, indeed, seemed far too mundane a word for what had happened to the fortunate world; nativity itself was hardly more than adequate. Little Wotan was not a baby, he was Baby; a quintessence of which all other babies were but flawed imitations.

Sober nurses swore he glowed at night…'

A year later:

'…He signed with Media Visualising Services Ltd to pose for six boarding posters, six full-page newspaper advertisements, and six 30-

second television commercials, for the greater glory, not to say sales, of Hartfelt Talcum Powder.

Which, within one week of the start of the little Wotan campaign, had become totally unobtainable anywhere in the United Kingdom, such was the volume of ecstatic customers hurling itself at the queendom's counters. For the first time in recorded cosmetic history women were buying tins of talcum powder by the gross.

And all that little Wotan Couchgrass had done to generate this frenzy had been to roll over twice and wriggle deliciously between a pair of unidentified hands.

He did even less to put Zugspitz Rusks into unprecedented profit. Since no one at the studios could prevail upon little Wotan to eat the revolting product, they settled for allowing him to stick it in his ear and laugh.

It was enough.

To celebrate his second birthday, little Wotan became Wograss Enterprises Ltd, discreetly registered in the Cayman Islands, and hired himself out to Media Visualising Services for the purpose of starring with a box of paper handkerchiefs. These he merely crumpled up and threw around, climaxing his act by waltzing with the empty box.

It started a fashion which took a full year to run its course. At one Manchester United home game alone, an estimated three tons of tissue balls were hurled from the terraces. The vogue, indeed, might have continued for ever, had it not been displaced by one which required its adherents to squirt toothpaste at one another, a trend commemorated by the Shineybrite Company with the gift of a heliotrope Lamborghini in which little Wotan was able to travel quickly and comfortably between personal appearances at major chemists.

By the end of that third year of little Wotan's life, the country's birth-rate had almost doubled. Not only did hitherto childless couples either renew their efforts or change their attitudes in the hope of producing an offspring as ineffably ideal as Wotan, but couples who already had children went once more to the uterine well in the hope of drawing thither a bucketful as wonderful as Wotan, who was, of course, superior

in every way to the examples they had previously produced.
He was everyone's dream-child.'

And so the success went on. The Couchgrass parents changed their family name to Lovelife, and founded a new company. Adverts featuring Wotan appeared regularly on commercial television:

'The Lovelifes were born. Since they were the property of Media Visualising Services Ltd, their screen debut involved only those items of babycare promoted by little Wotan. The world, previously captivated by fleeting and unconnected appearances of little Wotan, suddenly sat up, agog, to realize that what they would now be seeing was a continuous narrative of the growth to manhood of their tiny idol. They tuned to the commercial station first in millions, then in tens of millions, and before very long in all the millions there were.

By the end of the Lovelife family's first trading year, the British Broadcasting Corporation was operating out of two rented rooms above a Willesden fish-shop. Its executives, prematurely retired to rural almshouses, sat festooned in cobwebs, staring at the floor.

The Couchgrass family had prospered, too. The profits from little Wotan had enabled them not only to move from Primrose Hill to an eighteen-roomed house in Belgrave Square, but also to buy an entire Dordogne village of 31 cottages which they knocked together to form a holiday bungalow covering 16 acres.'

The Wotan story, you won't be surprised to hear, did not have a happy ending (although to discover how and why, you will need to do some research amongst newspaper back-numbers). However, this extract takes us back to our starting point.

The story's central themes are Wotan's total irresistibility, and his success in attracting the support of his adoring public. Any product to which his name was attached became a *must-have* item: something of whose existence everyone was aware; with which they wished to be associated; which no thinking person could, or would, do without. A product so utterly *irresistible*, that for parents it would be the very *last* thing that they would willingly forgo or give up.

The question for all of us is: How can we achieve the 'Wotan effect' for our schools – with our prospective and current parents and pupils, friends and potential donors alike? In marketing terms, how can we make education in our schools the *must-have* item, even more unthinkable to forgo than the more expensive home or holiday; the new car; Sky TV; a glass of good wine each evening; even private health insurance or golf club membership? And in development terms, the enterprise and project that financial supporters will continue to back even when they have to shed all the other causes that they once supported?

We hope this book has given you plenty of ideas about how the 'Wotan Effect' can be achieved and sustained.

© The Times and 31st January 1976 / nisyndication.com